Maxen Remembers

by

Mary Caragozian Thompson

authorHOUSE™

1663 LIBERTY DRIVE, SUITE 200
BLOOMINGTON, INDIANA 47403
(800) 839-8640
WWW.AUTHORHOUSE.COM

First published by AuthorHouse 2/6/2006

ISBN: 1-4208-9026-3 (sc)
ISBN: 1-4208-9025-5 (dj)

Library of Congress Control Number: 2005909148

Printed in the United States of America
Bloomington, Indiana

This book is printed on acid-free paper.

Dedication

This book is dedicated to the descendants of Maxen, the descendants of her three uncles and to generations to come

In Memory Of

My mother Maxen, father Armen, and brother John

Table of Contents

Acknowledgements

$\mathcal{T}$his book would not have been written without the encouragement and a great deal of input from my nephew, John Caragozian. The very foundation of this writing in the way of vital family information and history was kindly given to me by our family historian, George Aghjayan. My deepest gratitude goes to both John and George.

Love and appreciation goes to my son, Alan Thompson, who did the cover design and all the technical work.

My heartfelt thanks go to two dear, long-time friends: Emily Fawcett who offered helpful advice and perspective when I needed it and Elyse Mengle who twice scrutinized the manuscript.

Very special thanks to my sister Helene Caragozian- Webb who recalled many family happenings; to Ara Kefer who kindly supplied me with pertinent books, maps, and helpful information; to Edward Aghjayan and Hutch Aghjayan who gave me valuable information about their fathers, Kegham and Yezegeil. My appreciation to Johnnie Zaninovich, Nada Stuckey, Diane Bassett, Marion Killion, Armen Kandarian, John Atmajian and Sharyn Okino Kobashigawa and Krista Barrett for their remembrances. Great appreciation goes to Hal Myers who patiently taught me how to operate a computer and resolved the many problems I encountered thereafter. My deepest thanks to Genie Certain who proofread the manuscript, not once, but a second time after final revision.

Although my beloved brother John died suddenly in 1996, Part II of this story would not have been complete without his input. Through the years he had related family happenings to his son John and, after his death, more facts emerged through his short autobiography and the family documents he had saved.

MAXEN'S ESCAPE ROUTE TO AMERICA
1919-1920
(This map is approximate and not to scale)

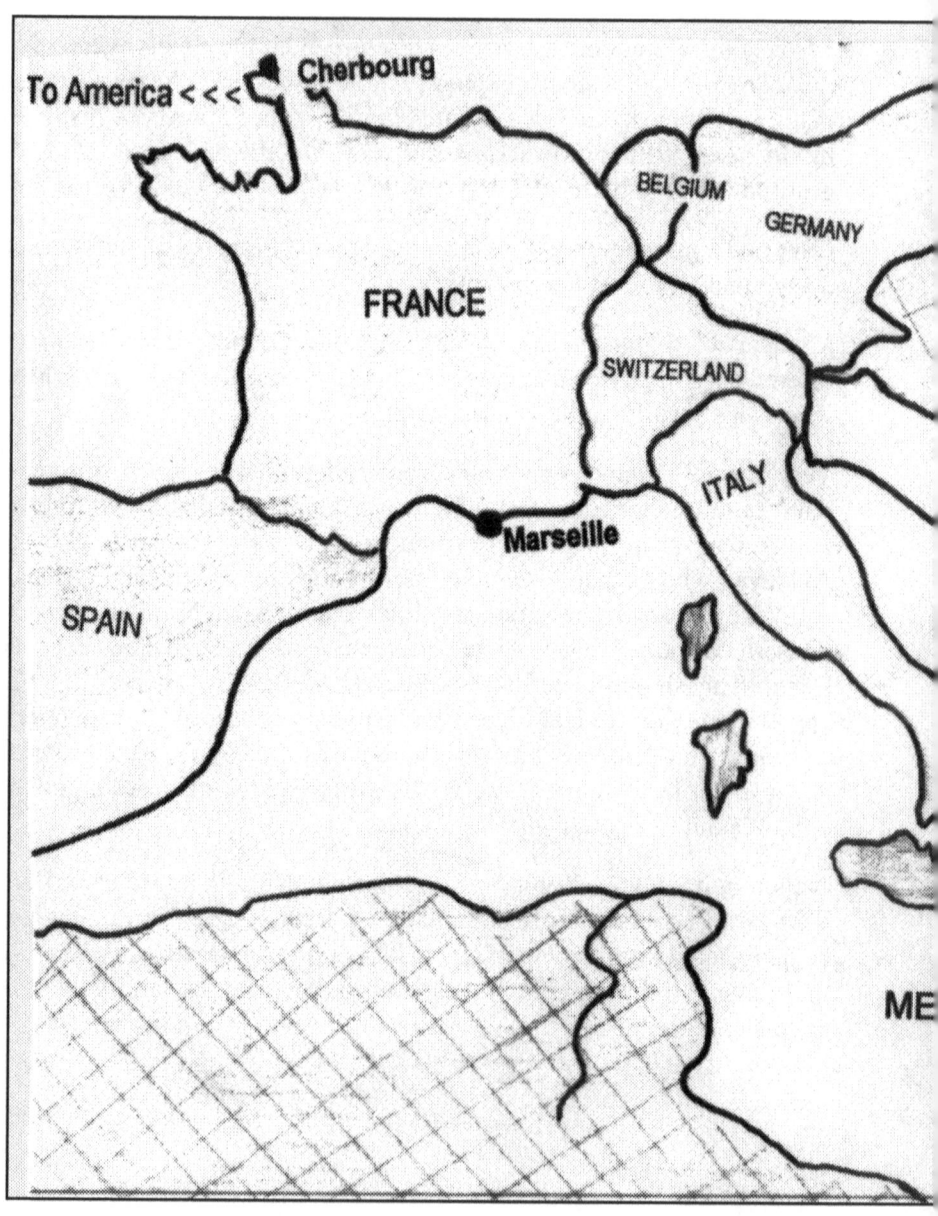

From her village of Burun Kishla, in the province of Yosgot, Turkey, Maxen fled south to Adana then to Mersine. By ship she traveled to Bierut, Lebanon and on to Marseille, France.

MAXEN'S ESCAPE ROUTE TO AMERICA
1919-1920
(This map is approximate and not to scale)

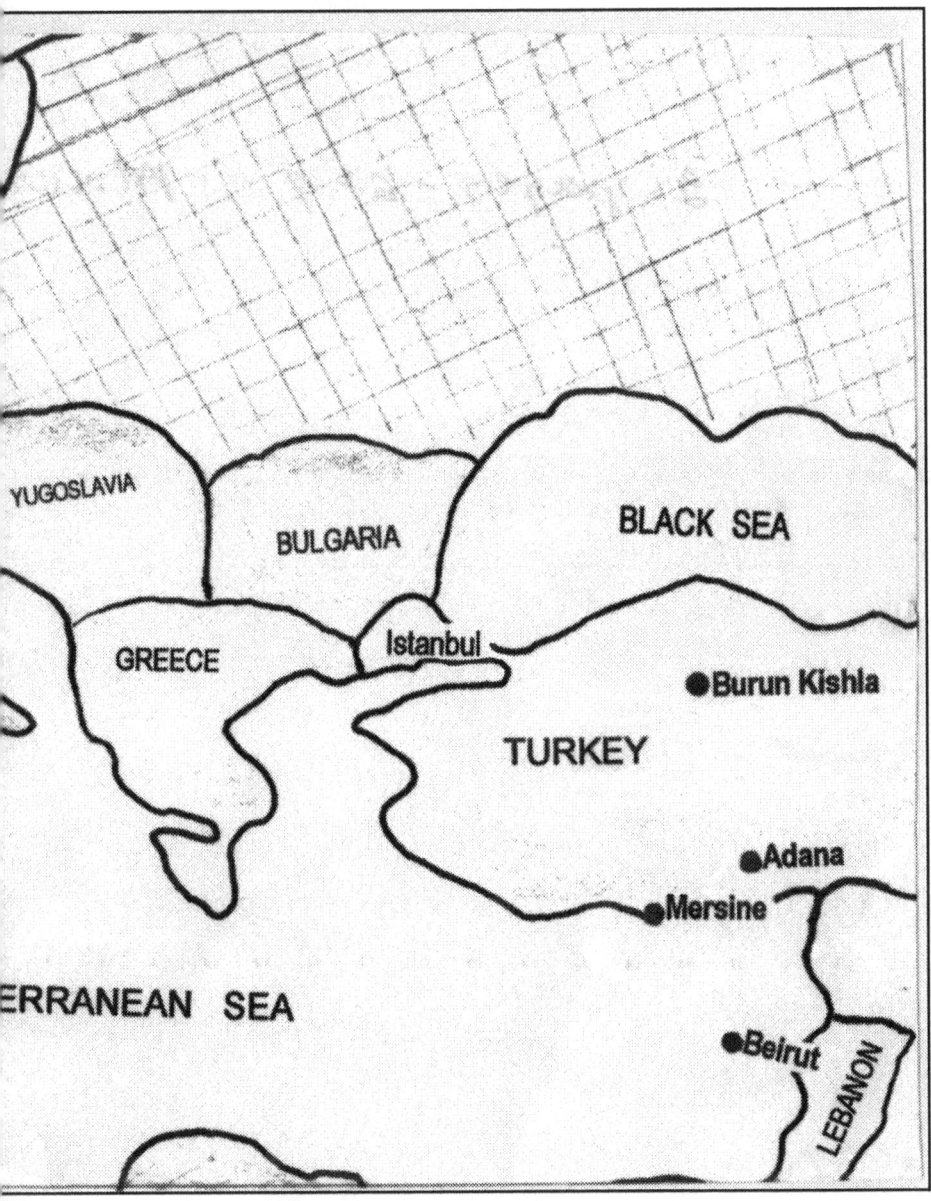

She rode a train to the port city of Cherbourg, France where she boarded a ship that took her to New York City in 1920.

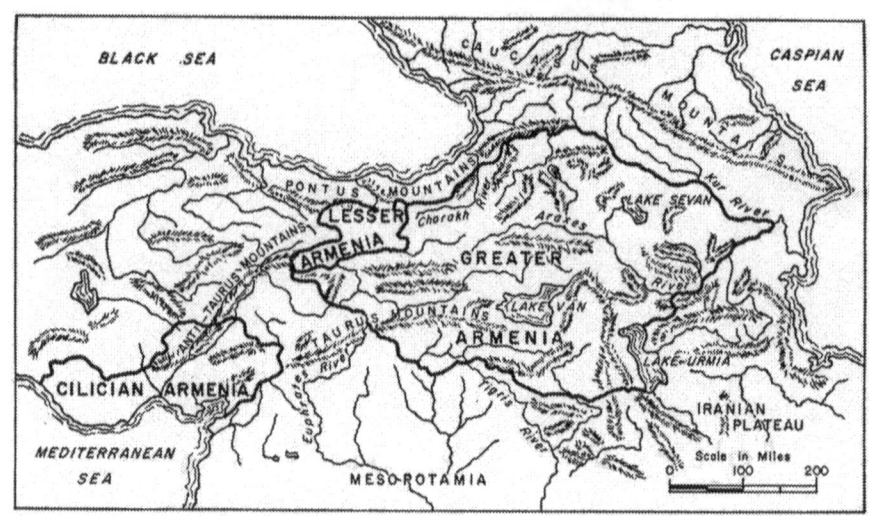

Historic Armenia once had an area of 100,000 square miles. Of its 2600 history there were 1022 years of self rule.

Present day Armenia, a tenth of its former size, is in southwestern Asia and is once again self-governing. Its capital, Yerevan, was founded in 800 B.C.

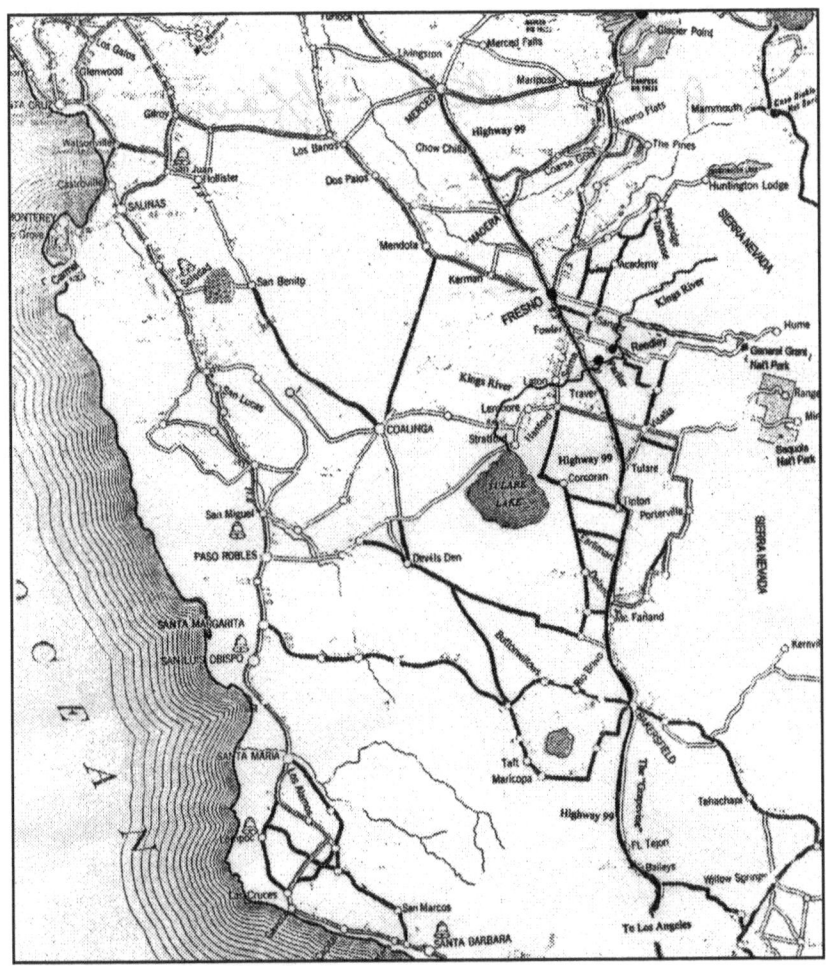

Central California, as it was when Maxen arrived in 1921. The Caragozian ranches were midway between Reedley and Parlier. General Grant National Park (where the Caragozians vacationed during the summers of the 1940's) became part of Sequoia-Kings Canyon National Park. Tulare Lake dried up.

Preface

This is a true story about a woman, Maxen Aghjayan Caragozian, who was born into an affluent and well-known Armenian family in what is now Turkey in 1905. When she was ten years old, Maxen was wrenched from a happy childhood to unimaginable horror and loss when every member of her family was murdered by the Muslim Turks. She was a survivor of the first holocaust of the twentieth century.

The book is a narrative of her perilous journey from the Armenian village of Burun Kishla, where Maxen's family had lived since the early 1700s, to California and of her life thereafter.

Maxen endured many tragic years of hardship, trauma and pain in her youth yet refused to let bitterness or resentment warp her outlook. She emerged as a strong, positive person with a keen intellect, a great sense of humor and many talents. She remained a constant source of love and encouragement for her children and an inspiration to her friends.

Forward

As a child I overheard conversations between my mother Maxen and her friends who had also survived the early twentieth century Armenian Genocide. They spoke about their lost world, recalling the happy years when they were growing up in the midst of loving families and of the nightmare that followed. They would wipe away the tears and change the subject when children were around. I felt their grief and wondered why these terrible atrocities had taken place and felt sadness in that my very own mother and others had experienced these agonies. Going about my untroubled young life, I pushed to the back of my mind what had happened "way back then" in the Old Country.

During my visits in my mother's final years, she talked at length about her happy childhood and described her house and family as well as her village and its people. She recalled Armenian customs and lifestyles during the early 1900's in the "Old Country." She talked about how her young life was abruptly changed to one of slavery in a Turkish household. I listened to the narration of her arduous country-to-country odyssey that led to America. She vividly described experiences, both good and bad, that had taken place in her life seven decades before.

It seemed unbelievable and truly amazing to me that my mother, even as an orphaned child, had roots of resilience, faith and courage so deeply embedded in her character that she was able to endure the unspeakable and still emerge whole. These same traits carried her through the difficult times in her adult life as well.

The realization that Maxen must be remembered through succeeding generations came after her funeral, when her oldest grandson said, "I feel sorry for future generations who will not know Grandma." This book is written in hopes that this remarkable woman and the ancient civilization from which she came will not be forgotten.

Part I One is Maxen telling her own story. Part Two is my perception of her life in the United States. The history within is my interpretation as written and told by others.

Mary Caragozian Thompson

Part One

Maxen Remembers

Chapter One

My Village

Our home was in a rugged, snow-capped mountainous terrain high on the Anatolian plateau of north central Turkey where no trees grew. At our elevation the weather was bitterly cold throughout the long winter. Each year we eagerly awaited the arrival of the warm spring and summer.

Spread like a fan below the village was a fertile valley where my family had large fields of grain, vineyards of grapes, orchards of fruit trees, and pastures where our sheep grazed. The blistering summer heat down in the valley was tolerable because it was necessary for the ripening of the different crops that grew there.

I was growing up, secure and contented, in the midst of a loving, well known family in the village of Burun Kishla where four to five hundred families lived together peacefully. Nearly all of the two thousand people there were Armenians except for a small number of Greeks and Turks. Our village was in the district of Yozghad which was in the province of Ankara in what was then the Ottoman Empire.

The men in our village had to travel quite a distance to the nearest city for needed supplies and for business matters. The two cities that were but a day's journey from us were Gesaria and Ankara. Gesaria, now called Kayseri, was preferred much of the time because the journey was a little faster and a bit easier. Mt. Ararat and Yerevan were quite a distance east of our village. Mt. Ararat, called the "cradle of civilization" and traditionally cited as the first landfall of Noah's Ark, is the area where Armenians have lived for over 2,600 years.

My grandfather usually traveled to the city by horseback, taking several donkeys along to carry the goods he would be bringing back with him. It took one day to go and one day to shop. On the third day the donkeys slowly followed him home, loaded down with long, sturdy sacks bulging with provisions. When I saw the donkeys trudging up the narrow mountain path to our village in the summer months, I knew there must be big, juicy watermelons in those heavy canvas bags. That was a fruit that was not grown in our area.

The melted snow from the mountains above and around us became streams of crystal clear water that flowed swiftly beside our village all year long. I was lulled to sleep at night listening to the soothing sound of water rushing over the rocks in the wide stream that ran close to our house. The abundant water was funneled through big pipes to wherever it was needed.

Chapter Two

My Family

I believe I was born in 1905, though it could have been 1904. I know I was born in the spring, because I was told that my mother went into birth labor while planting onions. She must have been in her late twenties when she died in 1913. It seemed to me that my mother brought forth a new brother or sister every year. I was the oldest child at eight years of age when she died. She left behind six children which included my three month old baby sister. I understood that my mother was gone forever and felt very distressed and sad. My three brothers and two sisters continued crying and calling for our mother for a long, long time. They just didn't understand why she had abandoned us.

I still wonder why she died. Maybe it was because she had so many children in such a short time—she gave birth to six babies in eight years. Midwives came to the house to help with the deliveries. We had no medical doctors or prescribed medicines to treat serious illnesses or injuries in our village. There were many long standing home remedies for minor illness, such as tea mixed with honey and herbs for colds. One life threatening illness at that time was typhoid fever, which was a rare occurrence when it happened in our village. Perhaps that was what killed my mother.

I knew my mother loved me but she didn't have much patience with me, most likely because I was so very active every minute of the day. I remember how annoyed she was when I would ask her one question after another. Now I realize how worn out she must have been caring for so many small children and coping with the never ending work.

5

My mother, Mariam Arslanian Aghjayan, was very pretty with her light brown hair and hazel eyes. Because she was petite and I was small for my age, the older folks told me I would most likely be like her when I grew up.

I believe I was my father's favorite child, probably because I was the oldest and I looked so much like him. We both had blue eyes and red hair. But my mother had told me that I looked like her two brothers whose eyes were the very same bright blue color as mine.

I knew my mother had five brothers and three sisters but I don't remember seeing any of them. My mother's parents and extended family lived in a small town that was some distance away. We didn't visit because it involved traveling through areas where the Kurds roamed, ready to rob and kill unsuspecting travelers.

My heart was full of love and pride for my father, Roustuni Aghjayan. Roustuni was a historical name and one used by noblemen in earlier times. Both my father and grandfather were greatly respected community leaders. My father was the spokesman (mayor) of the village and my grandfather was a magistrate within the province. It was easy to spot my father in a crowd because he was tall compared to the other men in the village; my grandfather was even taller.

Although I was a girl, (boys were favored in the Old Country) my father took time to do things with and for me. I called him *Hayrig,* a term of endearment which means daddy in Armenian. In the winter when the snow was deep he carried me to school on his shoulders. *Hayrig* laughed at the mischievous things I did while my grandmother scolded me for misbehaving.

I still remember how *Hayrig* put his head back when he laughed and all I could see was his chin and his red mustache. Most of the men in our village not only had mustaches but sported short, trim beards as well. The Armenian priests looked solemn and distinguished with their dark mustaches and long beards.

My father was the oldest son who, in our culture at that time, lived with his parents and inherited the house and land. His brothers were not left out. My grandfather and father were responsible for the well being of everyone in extended family. There was close communication between my grandfather and all his sons. Three of my father's bachelor brothers lived somewhere else but two married brothers had their homes and families in the village. He regularly sent money to the three brothers who lived elsewhere. Usually daughters and grand daughters were not a matter of concern because custom dictated that they marry at an early age and move to their husbands' household.

After my mother died, the whole workload of caring for the family of ten rested on my grandmother's shoulders. She single-handedly kept the household going. Her name was Nazley but we children called her *Medz Mirig* which means grandmother in Armenian. Even before my mother died, I was given the responsibility of caring for my younger brothers and sisters when I wasn't in school. I complained because I wanted to be playing with my friends. Each time I protested, *Metz Mayrig* looked at me sternly and said, "What you do is for me but what you learn is for you". Translation: you learn and gain experience by doing work. How true this was.

Medz Mayrig must have been continually exhausted because I don't remember her ever smiling. Many days she was up before dawn to make the flat bread, called *hatz or lavash* that we ate at every meal. After our breakfast she began cooking enough food for the next two meals. She served us ample food, cleaned the house, washed our clothes by hand, did the necessary chores and looked after us children. I wondered if she had any time left to sleep.

There was no indoor plumbing in the house. The water was brought inside for our use in big buckets made of wood and copper. Since there was no electricity, we used lanterns and candlelight at night. Our warmth in the winter came from a sunken fire pit, called the *tunir*.

When I was ten, my father married a teenage girl. She was not at all interested in taking care of us children and made no attempt to cook or to help my grandmother with the heavy work load. I don't know if she was just lazy or if she was too young to know how to do these things. My weary grandmother had yet another mouth to feed.

Large numbers of men in our village and elsewhere lived well into their eighties and nineties in good health. My father's grandfather lived one hundred and ten years. The women, on the other hand, died much younger. I don't remember seeing any old women in our village. The men out lived one or two wives and remarried very soon after being widowed.

We were a small family compared to some others in the village. There were households that had extended families of up to twenty in three generations living together. Often times there would be two brothers and their wives living in the same house with their children. While, most certainly, the grandfather of each household "ruled the roost", the grandmother supervised every day activities that went on in the house. There was no outward bickering or quarreling because every one understood their place in the family unit. Like it or not, this was the accepted and traditional way of life and had been through the centuries— generation after generation.

Chapter Three

The Valley

From our house we could see our vast fields of wheat. Lentils, that were used to make thick, tasty soups and stews, were planted in the middle of the wheat. There was also barley and millet growing along side the wheat. We had even larger fields of sweet smelling alfalfa, a dark green crop that was cut and dried into hay. The mounds of hay were taken up to the village for storage so that we could feed the large number of animals through the winter months.

There were times when my father allowed me to come down into the valley with him. I ran straight to the orchards, climbed the trees and ate my fill of the ripe, juicy fruit. I had my choice of peaches, plums, apricots, pomegranates, figs, apples or pears. Walnut and almond trees stood near by along with some olive trees.

I couldn't climb trees in our village because there weren't any. No trees could grow there because of the high elevation, harsh winters and the rocky terrain. I never saw a shade tree or pine tree until I left the area. The only trees I was familiar with were the fruit, nut and olive trees in the valley.

I could see acres of vineyards where our grapes grew. Although the soil was fertile and all the other crops grew plentifully, for some reason not many grapes hung on the vines. Perhaps the summers were too short. We ate the grapes fresh and dried, as raisins. A small portion of the grapes was made into wine and some raisins were put aside to make a potent liqueur called *raki*. These two beverages were served only on special occasions such as weddings and other celebrations.

A big patch of sugar cane was planted so we could have molasses to sweeten and flavor foods. Some of it was turned into a delicious confection we children loved to eat. The molasses was put in a large kettle, then simmered and beaten with a sturdy wooden paddle for a very long time. Gradually the dark syrup turned pale yellow in color and became very thick like soft taffy. The candy was given to us children only on special occasions.

My family hired workers who cultivated, watered and harvested the crops. I was not allowed to go in the small buildings that were in the middle of our vineyards because this is where the men lived. After the harvest, they pruned the fruit trees and grape vines and returned to the village to live through the late fall and winter months.

When my grandfather saw that we had harvested enough fruit and nuts for our family and relatives, he always invited villagers to come help themselves to what remained on the trees and the vines.

Boundary lines, dividing one property from another, had to be quite conspicuous and wide to avoid any squabbles among property owners. Keeping undesirable people out of the fields was another important reason for these sizeable borders. The dividers, made of waist high mounds of dirt and rocks, were the most common way of showing division of property. The dirt mounds were covered with thick, very thorny flowering bushes that would cause much pain for any trespasser who was foolish enough to climb over the divider. Entry gates to the property were kept locked at all times. These measures had to be taken because great numbers of fierce nomadic Kurds roamed the land and stole whatever they could.

Chapter Four

Sheep And The Sheep Dogs

Away from the orchards and vineyards were the grazing areas for the sheep. My family employed two shepherds who took care of the sheep. Only when the snows came were the sheep brought up to the shelters near our house. Once a day the sheep were taken from their winter shelters to drink from the troughs into which water flowed day and night.

Our big white sheep dogs were with the sheep the whole time they were out in the pastures. They watched over the sheep as they grazed during the day and patrolled the area all night while the shepherds slept. The dogs kept the hungry packs of coyotes, wolves and other animals away from the sheep, as well as thieves who were ready to snatch a lamb or two.

The sheep dogs were fierce to strangers—they allowed no one to come near the sheep except the shepherds and our family. When the dogs came back from the grazing areas to the village my father would say "Hurry and get these dogs into their pens." He was afraid they would attack someone. Once, a woman walking by our house tried to pet one of the dogs and was badly bitten on her arm. The big dogs were gentle with children, with the shepherds, and the adults in our family, but hostile to anyone else.

Although we had smaller dogs, we children liked to play with the sheep dogs. We had fun riding them as if they were horses. They were so big that my feet didn't touch the ground when I sat on their backs. The dogs were pure white with thick fur that was long and straight. They wore heavy leather collars circled with spikes to protect them against the wolves when they were in the fields.

It was said that we were the only family who had this breed of dog. For many, many generations, our family had bred and trained these big dogs to guard the sheep. Everyone in the province and beyond knew about them. Those who also raised sheep came from great distances to buy one of our dogs. My family sold, for a handsome sum, individual dogs when they were young but well trained.

We had a great many sheep—in the hundreds. The sheep and their wool were sold as income for our family. Making money was not the only reason the sheep were necessary. They were a source of food in our diets –we used lamb meat in many ways for our meals. Most important, too, was the rich milk sheep provided. We drank it and made it into a hard cheese, churned it into butter and made pans of *madzoon*.

What is now known as yogurt was called *madzoon* in my homeland. For countless centuries Armenians, Greeks and other Middle Eastern people have been making and eating yogurt. The adults drank a beverage called *tahn* which was simply yogurt diluted with cold water.

We children drank cow's milk in the summer when the sheep were out in the grazing lands and sheep's milk in the winter months when they returned to the village. I didn't like the taste of sheep's milk—I drank milk only in the summer months but ate soft and hard cheese the year round.

Our sheep also provided us with wool that was spun into yarn, used to make warm sweaters and coats, gloves, socks, shawls, and vests. Wool was also the material used for stuffing quilts and pillows and mattresses. Beautiful rugs of all sizes were made from wool yarns by those who were skilled in weaving.

Once a year the sheep were sheared. At that time numbers of poor people would gather nearby, quietly watching. Knowing they were in need of warm sweaters and thick quilts to see them through the bitterly cold winters, my grandfather gladly shared the wool with them.

My family had many other animals besides the sheep and dogs and a cow. We had camels, donkeys, oxen, water buffalos and horses.

Donkeys were needed to haul crops and goods in carts around the village and in fields. They seemed to know exactly where to go. Our handsome horses were for riding and hauling family and goods longer distances. Water buffalo were there for really heavy work because they had the most endurance. The toughest work of all was plowing the hard ground. Oxen were the animals for this job because they had the greatest strength of all the animals. And, of course, there were the camels.

Chapter Five

Aghjayan Camels

I really loved our camels. On command they would squat down so I could sit on them, just for fun. I didn't see them much because the camels did not stay with us. A man, an expert on camels employed by our family, was with them at all times as they traveled through the different provinces of the region. These big, morose animals, along with their keeper, were hired by merchants in various towns and villages for a substantial fee. Merchants and farmers   needed to take their goods to sell at other localities, so our camels were very much in demand.

There were no decent roads to speak of in the area—they were mostly side trails. What we called roads were mostly wide pathways joining place to place and were only wide enough for horse drawn carts. In the winter the routes of travel were covered with deep   snow and ice and were very treacherous to man and beast. Most of the roads were closed for nearly six months of the year.

At that time and place camels were used to move heavy goods from city to city, just as the trucks, trains and planes do now. It was the best and only way of transporting merchandise, especially in that terrain. Horses with wagons and donkeys were used to carry the lesser supplies in places with easier access. The sure footed camels, with their two toed cushioned feet had the endurance and strength to safely reach their destination no matter how harsh and icy the conditions. Another reason they were in high demand was that camels were very low maintenance and had high endurance. These tough animals were not at all particular as to what they ate and could go for days without water.

There was a time that my grandfather was the one who traveled with our fleet of camels as they took a large cargo of material to a far off city. He was robbed as he was coming back to our province, loaded down with the goods of another merchant. He also had the money for the materials he had just delivered. A few miles from his destination, a group of fierce Kurds swooped down upon him, taking every piece of merchandise that the camels were carrying. He was grateful that they didn't kill him and so relieved that they had overlooked a worn leather bag attached to an old donkey in the caravan. The big, heavy bag was filled with gold and money he was to give the merchant whose goods he had just delivered.

The Turks took possession of our camels in 1914, when I was nine. A few weeks later they came to the village and took our fine horses.

Chapter Six

The House And Garden

Right next to our house was the vegetable garden. Summers were short but the garden thrived because there was a rich layer of soil on top of the rocky terrain along with lots of sunshine and plenty of water. We either grew our vegetables or we did without, so every spring my mother or grandmother planted the garden from the seeds she had saved from the year before. By mid summer they began preparing the many kinds of vegetables for winter storage.

Planted in neat rows in our garden were eggplant, onions, carrots, peppers, garlic, potatoes, turnips, beets, cucumbers, Swiss chard, okra, potatoes, squash, zucchini and cabbage. There were many herbs whose sweet fragrance filled the garden space.

Some mornings we children were sent out to the garden to pick the flowers off the squash plants which were cooked into a tasty side dish. We would much rather have gone into the mountains to pick the beautiful wildflowers growing there but we were forbidden to do this because of the many dangers. There may have been wild animals but the real danger was much worse. Kurds roamed throughout the mountains and did not hesitate to kidnap or kill children.

My grandfather had once told me that throughout their history the Armenians never ventured into Kurdish territory. The Kurds lived in the impassable regions of the Taurus and other mountains and roamed the countryside. That they were *vayreni* (barbaric) was well known, and they were always at war.

Our house was not big by modern standards, but it was the largest one in the village. It was built to last through the generations. There was no moving from one house to another—no buying or selling. The family could repair or rebuild, but they would never sell their home—this was and had always been the Aghjayan's house.

I can't say the houses were attractive. They all looked alike and dull looking because there wasn't much choice of how you could build a house. Since there were no trees in our area, the building material had to be stonework and mud. The poorer families had adobe-like houses that were made mostly of dried mud. Our house and some others were made out of large stones, held together with large amounts of mud used as mortar and they were all one story.

The walls of our house were nearly two feet thick so there was plenty of insulation. The flat roof was built by laying heavy timbers from wall to wall. On top of these were placed smaller pieces of wood that was topped with a foot or two of packed down dirt that turned hard when it was mixed with water. There were channels in the mortar so the water and snow could be carried off by spouts beyond the eaves. We lived on one floor, with the dogs and the horses housed beneath us in the winter months.

The windows were small and high up on the walls, and there was no need for screens because we had no bugs. Most of the floor was also made of smooth, flat stones that were covered with large, colorful, hand-woven rugs.

We used kerosene lanterns and candles for light at night. The handmade candles were housed in four sided glass and brass candle holders that had handles so we could carry them with us when we went to our room at night.

The large main room in our house had the fireplace, eating area and comfortable built-in seating called *seders* which were used mostly in the warmer months. Our family liked to sit around the *tunir* fire pit on rugs or large pillows during the cold winter.

In a corner of the main room was a small cylinder shaped cabinet made of wood and brass that was used to store the china demitasse cups and saucers along with coffee and sugar. It was kept locked to keep us children out. I checked that cabinet door often and when it was left unlocked I reached in and quickly popped a sugar lump into my mouth.

There were also rooms for sleeping but the most important room was toward the back of the house—the storage room where all the food for the winter was stored. It was also locked and the key stayed in my grandmother's apron pocket. We understood why this room was a forbidden area to us children. I, along with my siblings, many cousins and friends, would be in there eating, playing and making a mess if we could get in there.

Some times my tired grandmother took a nap. Knowing I was the daring one, my cousins and my brothers would beg me to sneak the key from her pocket so they could get into the store room to eat some of their favorite things. I can't believe I was talked into committing theft for the others, but I did.

I would slowly and carefully take the key from her apron pocket, open the door, and stand guard while they ate their fill. When my siblings and cousins ran out of the store room, I hurriedly locked the door and quietly returned the key. I think my grandmother noticed a difference when she went into the storage room, but she didn't say anything.

Walking into the storage room was a wonderful experience because it smelled so good. Each neatly stored in a certain place, every food had its own fragrance. There were herbs, dried fruits, nuts, jams, dried beans; molasses and honey in earthen jars. This room had a dirt floor that served a purpose. Huge cabbages, carrots, beets, turnips and potatoes were buried in the cold dirt for winter storage. These vegetables were dug up as needed, washed well and cooked into many tasty dishes.

Onions, used in most of our Armenian dishes, were braided and hung on the storage room wall. Even toward the end of winter, the tops were still green with only a tinge of yellow. Different kinds of cheeses that were packed in airtight sheep skin pouches were also hung on the wall for cool storage.

Along with the cheese and onions were cured meats carefully hung and used as needed all winter and spring. The two most popular ones were called *basterma,* which was dried beef, and *soujough,* which was more like a very dense sausage. Both were prepared by using plenty of salt, spices and garlic, then stored in a cool place. They were cut into thin slices and eaten as appetizers or perhaps as the meat for a light meal.

I knew exactly where one of my favorite treats, called *rogig,* was stored. *Rogig* was and is made by stringing together two foot lengths of whole walnut halves. A big pot of grape juice was put on the fire to simmer for hours until it became thick. The long strings of walnuts were dipped into the syrup and dried in the sun then dipped and dried again many times until the coating was a half inch thick. To serve, it was cut into half inch slices that were chewy hard on the outside and crunchy with walnuts on the inside.

The storage room had three big wooden storage bins that were about seven feet high and four feet wide. There was a small door on the bottom of each bin to scoop out however much was needed of the different types of whole grains stored within. Often times it was my job to bring my grandmother the grains and whatever other food she needed that day to cook our meals.

The families took their grain to the local mill to be processed. Each family had an assigned time to do this. First, the bran (outer layer) was taken off the kernels of wheat and barley with the help of a wheel driven by a donkey. The grain was washed, boiled in huge cauldrons and spread on big sheets to dry in the sun. This step was necessary to make the grain easier to cook. After drying, the *buglour (*wheat) was cracked into coarse or fine particles and used in making pilaf and various other dishes.

Butter made from the rich sheep's milk was stored in wooden buckets and used generously for cooking and baking. Made from milk that was poured into big pans, it was left overnight so the thick cream would rise to the top, leaving skim milk on the bottom. The heavy cream was put in a pot and stirred with a paddle until the solids separated from the liquid whey. After the whey was removed, the soft yellow butter was pressed down firmly into special storage buckets.

What work and organization it must have taken for the women to have prepared and readied the vast amounts of food to last a big family through the long winter months. There were no shortcuts, no modern conveniences and no outside help as they did this. The enormous and necessary job remained much the same through generations of women.

We children were fed a simple breakfast of cheese and bread with some fresh or dried fruit along with milk or yogurt as snacks during the day. We had hearty meals at noon time and leftovers for the evening meal.

Our main dish quite often had been cooking in an earthen pot for hours before we ate. Frequently it was a combination of wheat kernels, shredded lamb or chicken and vegetables. No meal was complete without bread and a bowl of *madzoon (*yogurt*)*. Desserts were only served when we had company.

The *tunir* fire pit was the central and most important part of our home all year around. Not a traditional fireplace, the *tunir* was a large circular, ceramic-type appliance that was sunk into the ground and used for all the baking and cooking and for warmth. It was lit very early every morning. A metal sheet or iron crossbars were put on top for baking and cooking all the meals for the day. After the cooking was done, the fire pit was covered with a round, low table-like fixture that allowed the heat to radiate throughout the room.

Since there was no heat in the bedrooms, we children would run to our rooms at bed time to bring back mats to lie on and thick quilts to cover us. We positioned ourselves around the *tunir*, with our feet toward the heat and slept—warm and comfortable. During the summer months we all went to our bedrooms to sleep.

Near the house there was the *oda (*pavilion*)* where my grandfather and father socialized with relatives and friends during the nice weather. The large gazebo-like structure had bulky, colorful cushions on the floor for the men to sit on while they visited. This place was only for men. Children knew they shouldn't be there; women were absent because their never-ending work did not allow any spare time for leisure.

I managed to be right there with the men, sitting cross legged on the floor and listening to their conversations as they ate appetizers and drank their strong coffee in little china cups. When my father asked me to collect and wash the demitasse cups, I would smile sweetly as I left the *oda* with a tray of cups and saucers. When I was out of sight, I stuck my finger in the bottom of a cup to taste the sweet coffee residue. Afterward I hurried back to the pavilion where my uncles slipped me a coin or candy –probably to get rid of me. Satisfied, I would race off to play with the other children. We jumped rope, chased each other around, played hide and seek, sang songs and entertained ourselves quite well.

We children addressed my parents' close friends as Uncle and Aunty. We didn't use their first or last names along with the title of Uncle or Aunty. Addressing them as such was considered a sign of respect and to indicate the closeness of their relationship to the family. The adults formally addressed each other as *Baron* (Mr.) and *Digin (*Mrs.*)* and their first names. Only close friends and relatives called each other by their first names.

Chapter Seven

School

*W*hen the snow was so deep that I couldn't walk to school, my father would hoist me on his shoulders and carry me. We both wore warm knitted hats on our heads and thick leather shoes. We girls wore dresses or skirts and blouses with bulky sweaters to keep us warm. My long hair was sometimes braided with ribbons on the ends when my grandmother had time to do it, but it usually just hung down my back.

There were no public schools. The private school in the village was a two story stone structure attached to the back of the church. There were about fifty boys and girls enrolled at the primary school. The girls' small classroom was upstairs and the boys' large classroom was on the ground level. Boys and girls were always in separate places, while studying and while playing. The secondary school was a separate building but also located near the church.

When I looked out the small window I could see the cemetery right next to the church, with the many crosses standing in rows and stone monuments covering the ground. It was the burial ground for all the Armenians who had died in the village, which included many, many generations of Aghjayans.

The student's family needed to provide everything for their classes. This meant a table and chair, pencils, paper, books and even fuel for the stove. My father always made sure the stove was putting out plenty of heat. Those who did not bring fuel had to sit away from the stove.

Our village school master was a well educated and respected person. You can be sure he never had a problem with discipline in the classroom. The language spoken and written was not Armenian but Turkish as mandated by the government officials. Everyone in the village spoke Turkish, even at home. I didn't learn how to speak Armenian until I left our province.

Formal education at that time was available to a select few. Less than one third of the children in our village went to school. Families who were more prosperous sent their boys to school and there were very few girls who attended. Students who showed special aptitude would be sent to larger cities that had colleges or to Europe to continue their education if their families could afford it.

I loved school, learned things in a hurry and stayed on top of our class. My father was aware of this, and he knew that I was teaching my boy cousins who didn't learn as fast. He assured me often saying, "My daughter, you will continue your education. I will send you to Talas where you will attend the American college." The college was on the outskirts of Gesaria. I had decided at the age of nine that I was going to be a teacher.

It was a matter of pride that all girls in the village knew how to do needlework. I was impressed when my mother told me that needlework lace adorned the garments of Armenian Queens way back before the Turks conquered Armenia. She also told me that Armenian lace is unique and different from any other. A needle and thread was all that was needed to produce unique patterns. The method of knotting the thread into a beautiful design was the basis of the lace and doily making. The girls my age went to a class to learn the technique of this intricate art. Most of us did sit still long enough to learn the basics. It was very time consuming; the more delicate the lacework, the longer it took to complete. The delicate lace represented the fineness and beauty of life in our rural setting. Oftentimes even simple dresses that women wore had a trim of this lace around the collar.

An example of Armenian knotted lace worked with a needle and fine thread, using a unique technique that dates back at least two thousand years. Maxen learned the basics as a child and made dozens of these intricate doilies, adding her special creative design to each one. They varied in size from six inches in diameter to twenty four inches. Many are now framed and cherished by her children and grandchildren.

Chapter Eight

Family Life In The Happy Times

At home we were taught to honor and love our elders. There was no back-talk from us children, only obedience. We understood that our family life was based on love and respect, one for another. Good manners, common courtesy, openhandedness and family values were ingrained into us by our mother and grandmother. I never learned any vulgar words because there were none spoken in our house.

When tasks and supper were finished we all sat around the *tunir*. We found entertainment in simple yet enjoyable ways. In our remote mountainous setting we had no concerts, sporting events, plays or any other diversion. In the early 1900's there were neither radios nor movies. It was the era of self entertainment, telling stories, fables and jokes, singing and playing games and gathering with friends to celebrate numerous events.

Our door was always open to visitors—hospitality and geniality was the way of life for our family. Getting together with other families was usually spontaneous, as friends would drop by just to chat. I could hear my father telling funny stories and everybody laughing. My mother or grandmother would bring out a variety of appetizers for our friends to enjoy.

The mark of hospitality and generosity was, among other things, serving an abundance of good food to visiting friends or relatives. The hostess didn't just put the food on the table, but urged her guests to have some of everything. Afterward she passed each dish of food around again to make sure everyone had enough to eat. It was considered extremely bad manners for guests to help themselves. The hostess must first invite and implore them to eat as she passed the different foods.

Guests were offered a strong, traditional beverage of finely ground coffee that was combined with sugar and water then heated in a special brass hourglass shaped brass coffee maker called a *jazveh*. After the coffee mixture came to a boil, it was carefully poured into the dainty demitasse cups. Often times, after finishing the coffee, the china cup was turned upside down on the saucer. One person would offer to look at the markings of the grounds inside the cup and "tell one's fortune". I listened intently to what was said and wanted my fortune told, or better yet, I wished I could be the one telling fortunes.

When it was a planned-ahead gathering, we had a fine time as we played games, told stories, played musical instruments, sang, and munched on tasty Armenian food. There was fun and much laughter for the men and children but not for the women.

During these times of leisure, the women usually would carry on with household tasks such as spinning, sewing, mending, weaving, embroidering or preparing food. Even as a child I noticed there didn't seem to be any rest or play for the women. No wonder they died so young.

I also noticed that toward the time I was ten, there was no longer any laughter or singing when friends came over. There would be quiet, serious talk as the children were sent off to another room. I know now they were fearful about the worsening situation and the imminent danger from the Turks. My father's face was no longer jovial and I noticed that the older people all looked very sad. I didn't understand why the women were crying.

Chapter Nine

Armenian Apostolic Church

Our family and most of the Armenians within our village belonged to and were closely connected with the Armenian Apostolic Church. Only fifteen village families were Protestant.

Apostolic means the church can trace its roots back to the apostles who came to Armenia to spread the word of Christ. Armenia was the first nation in the world to make Christianity its state religion in 301 A.D. St. Gregory, the Illuminator, persuaded Tiridates III, King of Armenia, to accept the faith. The first Christian church of the world was built in 303 A.D. by St. Gregory and began services. What was to become the Armenian Apostolic Church was born and became the center of life for Armenians. Our church served to keep alive not only our religion but also Armenian history, culture and language.

Our daily living habits and the laws of the church fit together nicely. The solemn church service was called the Divine Liturgy, *"Badarak"*, which resembles High Mass in the Catholic Church and was offered every day. It lasted nearly two hours with readings from the Holy Bible, chanting, singing and many prayers.

The church was most important in that it held us all together as a community. We were devout Christians living in a Muslim country. Since the Turks conquered Armenia hundreds of years ago, there had been inborn hatred toward the Christians living in their midst. The Muslim Turks looked upon all Christians as dogs or swine. No matter how bad the situation was, our church and strong family bonds gave us hope. Through hundreds of generations, the church was both our identity and our security.

Our village church, called Mother Mary of God Apostolic Church, was a sturdy rock structure built in the traditional and unique architecture of all Armenian churches. The rock walls were a good two feet thick—our churches were built to last hundreds of years through earthquakes, harsh weather or possible enemy attacks. The smooth stone floors were covered with beautiful hand woven rugs and the altar was graced with lovely hand knotted lace linen. There were twinkles of light on the gleaming gold filigree of the crosses and chalices on and above the altar. Incense, *khung,* was dispersed a few times during the service by the deacons who walked up and down the aisles chanting and swinging the brass metallic burners, *purvars,* up and down.

Men and women didn't sit together. The men sat, kneeled or stood on one side of the church and the women were on the other side.

Our priest dressed simply in a long black tunic and black head gear that had a pointed top. He had the respect and love of everyone in the village, young and old alike. As with other Eastern Orthodox clergy, Armenian priests—though not the bishops and other high churchmen—could marry. We called our priest *Der Hayr* and his wife was called *Yeretsgeen Mayr. Hayr* means father in Armenian and *Mayr* means mother. This title was given to all the Armenian clergymen and their wives.

Unfortunately, this dedicated, intelligent, educated man, Garabed Arzoumanian, was quite poor. He must have lived on faith because he received no pay for his seven days a week services. The only money the priest made was what was given to him for performing wedding ceremonies, blessing houses and doing baptisms and funerals. The villagers gave him vegetables from their gardens and were considerate of his needs.

I would sometimes go behind our priest and tug on his smock, just for the fun of it. He would turn his head to me and say, "My child, be careful. This (his wearing apparel) must last me a long time," and he would smile at me.

There was a second priest in the church who was much younger. He assisted the older priest and was a teacher at our secondary school. His name was Sarkis Geokjian. There was also a retired priest in our village whose last name was Arslanian, which was my mother's family name, but I don't know if we were related.

The Oldest Christian Church in the World

HOLY ETCHMIADZIN, THE MOTHER ARMENIAN CHURCH. The cathedral was built in 303 A.D., two years after the ruler of Armenia, King Trdat III (or Drtad) proclaimed Christianity as state religion. Armenia became the first Christian kingdom of the world. The ancient cathedral is located near Armenia's modern-day capital, Yerevan.

Chapter Ten

How We Dressed

*T*he clothes we wore everyday were simple both in fabric and style. The material was bought in Gesaria or Ankara and made into clothing by the women in the winter months when tasks were fewer. The type of fabric depended on the season of the year and how much the family wanted to spend.

The women wore dresses all year long, as did the girls. The men wore homespun shirts with jodhpur-type pants and boots and the boys dressed in a similar fashion. Men, women and children wore heavy hand knit sweaters in the cold weather rather than coats. We all wore sturdy leather shoes necessary for the rough terrain and the cold winters. Mothers and grandmothers wore wool scarves over their heads for warmth when they ventured outdoors during the winter. We children had knit hats to keep our ears warm. Everyone in the village wore plain, practical clothes as they went about their daily activities. In the summer we children liked to go barefoot whenever and wherever we could.

Dressing for weddings and other celebrations was quite another matter. These were the times that the women brought out their nicest clothes and jewelry as in elaborate rings, gold filigree bracelets and heavy gold necklaces. The women who could not afford gold wore ornate silver belts and pretty silver jewelry. I remember some of my mother's gold jewelry shining with dark red gems and deep green gems that must have been rubies and emeralds.

The really fine clothes were tailored in Ankara. For these special occasions, men sometimes wore suits or they wore trousers and vests with finely textured long sleeved shirts. The women wore matching skirts and blouses or dresses made of fine fabrics, silks and brocades. Those who could not afford fine dresses wore the best they had. In our village children did not dress up in fancy clothes.

Chapter Eleven

Celebrations

*H*olidays were celebrated in a big way in our village. There were many festivities: weddings, christenings, engagements, Christmas and Easter. On top of the list, the biggest and most important celebrations were Easter and weddings. We also celebrated Name days, honoring the saints and biblical figures instead of birthdays for family members. There was no such thing as a birthday party for child or adult.

Our Christmas celebrations were quite different than those in America. Most important was the fact that Armenians and other Eastern Orthodox people, observed Christmas on January 6th. We did not exchange gifts; we did not have a Christmas tree; there was no Santa Claus or stockings hung up to be filled; we did not decorate the house. The men and women of the village observed Christmas by fasting the day before. After Christmas Eve service at the church the fast was broken with a family meal. Christmas day was a commemoration and celebration of the birth of Christ. The adults went to church again and gathered afterward in fellowship of family and friends. We children got together to sing Christmas songs and were given sweets as a special treat.

New Years Day was a time for families to visit each other and to wish each other a happy new year. There was no New Year's Eve celebration.

Baptism was another happy occasion. After the church service relatives and friends gathered at the home of the baby's godparents for a big feast. The celebration continued through the afternoon with singing and dancing.

Funerals, on the other hand, were very simple and without big ceremony. Rich or poor, the dead person was taken from home to his or her final resting place in this same manner: the body was washed and completely wrapped with many yards of unbleached muslin or a shroud. Usually four men carried the body on a wooden slab or in a very simple coffin to the cemetery next to the church. They would place the body in the prepared excavation and cover it with dirt. The priest would deliver a short eulogy and that was it.

Chapter Twelve

Easter

I could always tell Easter was near because there was excitement in the air as activities began at home. The grown ups had much work to do in getting everything ready for this very important event.

The inside walls of our house were repainted white weeks before Easter. My father took all the big copper pots to the place where they were shined and reworked. The rugs were taken up and cleaned by kneading snow into them along with soap, then shaking it all out. Everything inside and outside the house was spruced up. New clothing was made for us children to wear at the Easter celebration.

The women began baking special desserts long before Easter. My mouth would start watering as I smelled the baking of *katah,* sweet yeast bread, *khorabia,* butter cookies, and the many layered *paklava* and other delicacies. After the breads and pastries were baked, the cooking of main dishes began. There were cubes of lamb meat marinating for the *shish kebab* that would be cooked over an open fire on *shishes,* skewers. Along with the kebabs would be plenty of rice pilaf, cooked vegetables, and side dishes.

All the Easter eggs were one color—a reddish copper brown, red being the traditional orthodox Easter color. Weeks before Easter the women began saving the outer peelings of red onions for the purpose of dying the eggs. When it was time, all the onion skins were put into a big pot of water to simmer along with the eggs. We children thought the colored eggs were so beautiful and they were tasty with a slight hint of onion.

The most important part of Easter was the church service—the observance of Christ's death and His Resurrection. The solemn eulogy lasted over two hours and was given several different times during the day. Every adult Armenian in the village first went to church and later joined the others for the celebration.

Long before Easter a certain place had been chosen where the families would gather after church. The rich and poor, the young and old would all be there Easter Sunday afternoon. Every family brought a plentiful supply of delicious food. Joy and laughter filled the air as we celebrated with singing, dancing, and feasting for two or three days. We children had such fun playing games while the grownups visited, danced, and sang. We went home to sleep and continued the celebration the next day.

Easter would not be Easter without the traditional sweet bread *katah*. A silver or gold coin was hidden in the dough before the bread was baked. The poorer families put a button in their *katah* instead of a coin. Some time during Easter day, the bread was cut into as many pieces as there were family members. The one who had the piece of bread containing the coin or button was destined to have good luck the rest of the year. The lucky person was congratulated and envied at the same time. This tradition of a coin in the bread was repeated on Christmas day.

Another exciting and fun activity was the egg cracking contest. Both children and adults came to the place of celebration with plenty of hardboiled eggs. The children, especially, couldn't wait to get started. The moment would arrive when everybody went around trying to crack the other's egg—end to end, not the middle of the egg. The folklore was that the darker eggs were the hardest. The last person with an unbroken egg became the winner.

The Easter celebration was a good time for girls and boys, who were of marriageable age, to discretely look around. The boys and girls glanced at each other but were not allowed to socialize. Often times this was the only way a young man would spot the girl who he would marry at a later time.

Chapter Thirteen

Weddings

Weddings, without a doubt, were the most drawn out, most important affairs for the family and for the people in the village. The customs and the rituals used in our village had been going on in the same way through the centuries.

Oh, how I loved to go to a wedding. I was usually the first one there. I took in every little detail of the happenings from beginning to end.

A girl had no say in choosing her husband—her opinion was never asked or considered. The marriage was arranged by both sets of parents. There was no romance or courtship as you see in modern times.

For the most part, each family knew the other family's qualities and shortcomings, since they had lived in the same area for many generations. Matches were made involving girls and boys outside the village also. My mother was from another village quite a distance away. They didn't take any chances on the suitability of the prospective bride or groom's family. The status of the family mattered a great deal. The wealthy families united their children to other wealthy families. My mother's family was quite influential and prosperous as was my father's family. I don't know how they knew about each other, but the two families pledged my mother and father in marriage.

It made a difference in marriage arrangements as to how many daughters there were in the family. The father couldn't be too picky about a prospective groom if he had half a dozen girls. For a girl to become older and not marry was considered a shame both to her and to her family. Also younger sisters could not marry until the older sister or sisters were married.

Close relatives were not allowed to marry each other. It went without saying that an Armenian girl would never marry a Muslim Turk.

Many times a boy's mother played a very important role in choosing her son's wife. The bridegroom, *Pesa* in Armenian, learned everything about the girl through his mother. As the future mother-in-law, she had to love her daughter-in-law as much as her own son since they would all be living together. She would make it her business to find out everything she could. If the boy's mother didn't approve of her, there was no marriage. If she liked the girl and her father consented, the marriage took place and lasted until the death of either partner.

In our village and elsewhere, the words "divorce" and "infidelity" were unknown. To have one of these happen would be a most terrible disgrace to the family.

When the choice of a bride was decided by the young man and his family, the boy's father came to the girl's father, on behalf of his son, to formally ask for the hand of his daughter. The girl's father had to make a choice—should he or shouldn't he "give" his daughter to them. He couldn't answer until he asked his daughter's godfather his opinion—the final word came from him. If both father and godfather approved of the match, the engagement ritual began.

At the time of the engagement the parents of the intended groom brought a valuable gift to the bride to be. The engagement was official when the groom's father gave the bride's father a ring for his daughter to wear until the wedding. Another ring was fashioned for the wedding day. If the groom's family couldn't afford two rings, they borrowed one for his intended to wear until the wedding. At the time the ring was given, small gifts were sent to the girl by her future mother-in-law.

The engagement lasted at least six months. Perhaps the pair saw each other after the engagement but they were never left alone. When one of them was from another village, the bride saw the groom for the first time on the wedding day.

The time during the engagement was often sad, rather than happy, for the bride-to-be and her sisters. Soon she would be leaving them to join another family. But who had time to cry? They needed to start working on filling the bridal "hope chest" with handcrafted gifts that were to be given to the groom's family. As soon as the engagement was official, the prospective bride's father hurriedly made or bought a large wooden chest for his daughter

The bride-to-be had a long list of the many different things she was to create: pillow cases, doilies, bedspreads, towels and even rugs. In addition she needed to make shawls, gloves, socks, scarves and aprons. This meant hours and hours of nonstop sewing, knitting, embroidering and lace-making. It was very important that she show her future in-laws how skilled she was in her handiwork.

Because it would have been an impossible undertaking for the future bride to fill the chest in these few months, the whole family was recruited. Her grandmother, mother, aunts and sisters all worked hard and long to help her make these many beautiful and practical items. When the chest was full, a special day was set aside for relatives and friends to come and admire all the handwork.

Along with the frenzy of sewing and knitting, there was the wedding dress and trousseau to think about. If the family could afford it, the bride and her father made a special journey to Gesaria or Ankara to have it made for her.

Wedding dresses were tailored with beautiful fabrics in colors of green, blue, turquoise or burgundy. I remember the pretty deep blue dress the girl wore when she married my father. The fabric for the wedding dress was usually velvet or brocade with embroidery and trim and a cape accompanied the dress. The head piece was a heavy bandana-like veil with gold threads or small ornaments sewn into it. This veil completely covered the bride's face.

The groom's family, not the bride's, had the responsibility of putting on the big wedding which included the church ceremony, the wedding feast and all the festivities after the ceremony. Because more than half of the villagers came to the wedding, planning and doing all this was a giant task. The groom's family needed to provide not only an abundance of good food and drink for the two day celebration but also musicians and singers. They needed to see about chairs and tables, big pots for cooking, plates and eating utensils. The huge pots and plates were rented from the church, as were some tables and chairs. Borrowing and renting were not only acceptable but a necessity in order to feed all the well wishers who would come. Fortunately, people came and went at different times so there were smaller groups eating rather than hundreds at a time.

The groom's family didn't need to extend special   invitations for the wedding feast. Every family friend and relative in the village knew about it and would be there. Wedding gifts were not a worry for the guests. The customary gift given to the bride by all the well wishers was gold.

Since the wedding celebration lasted two and sometimes three days, preparing for the feast was a huge undertaking. Relatives and neighbors were expected to come to the groom's house to help bake and cook the vast amounts of food that took weeks to prepare.

Instead of a wedding cake, traditional sweets were served: candy coated almonds that were wrapped up, tied with a ribbon and given away to the guests; the many layered *paklava,* delicate cookies called *kurabia* ; candy made with sesame seeds called *halvah*; candied apricots and figs and other delicacies.

When it was time for the baking of bread, eight to ten women gathered together to make *yogha,* a thin Armenian bread. They made the dough, rolled it out into thin sheets. After the bread was made, it was piled one on top of another in stacks that rose three or four feet high.

Huge cooking pots were brought in to be used for the cooking of the main dishes. These pots were so big that I could have easily sat in one and no one would have seen me. One of the big pots was used for lamb stew that was made with cubes of lamb, potatoes, onions, carrots, all well seasoned and simmered together a long time. The delicious stew was served on top of big mounds of rice *pilaf,* which required another giant pot.

There were many other delicious Armenian dishes for the hundreds of guests to enjoy. There was an overabundance of food because it would have been a terrible humiliation for the groom's family if there wasn't enough for everyone.

The bride's godmother played a big role in the wedding rituals. Her most important job was to lead the bride around because her gold-covered headpiece was so heavy that she couldn't see through it. The groom and the godmother were on either side of the bride as they walked her to the church for the wedding ceremony.

Musicians dressed in bright vests walked along side the couple playing happy dance music. The music was wonderful but what interested me the most was the dancing of the two frisky young men who were on each side of the *harss* and *pesa*, bride and groom. With a dagger in each hand, they twirled, leaped up in the air, dancing fancy steps all the way to the church.

Walking behind the bridal pair and the dancers were family, other relatives, and a few friends. The long procession filed into the church for the long wedding ceremony. We children were expected to wait outside. I couldn't wait for the ceremony to be over so we could go to the groom's house and start having some fun.

Finally the same family procession walked happily out of the church. I couldn't see the bride's face because she still wore the heavy veil. Once again, she was led and this time to the groom's house. It seemed to me that musicians accompanying them were playing louder and faster. What fun it was to watch the two young men with the daggers who danced even better and leaped much higher than before.

Before the feasting began, the bride's godmother led her to the various pots of food so she could sprinkle a little salt into each one, as was the custom. Still veiled, the bride stood up the whole time while friends and relatives congratulated her and gave her gifts of gold. Because she couldn't see anything, I wondered how she knew who gave her the gold and what the amount was.

The merriment continued with enthusiastic eating, drinking, dancing, singing and visiting for two days. Food was sent to those who were unable to attend the wedding festivities.

We children had a wonderful time those two whole days. We were free to roam, play, dance and eat whatever we wanted, whenever we wanted it. We spent our time stuffing ourselves on the appetizers and desserts, we listened to the musicians sing and play happy music and watched the grownups dancing around in a circle. Sometimes we would go where nobody could see us and practice dancing. Weddings were even more fun than our Easter celebration.

The groom was having a good time too. He was at the *Oda* where only his men friends and relatives came to greet and congratulate him. I sometimes watched as they sat on the handmade rugs and cushions and drank wine and brandy served to them by the groom. They laughed and talked and seemed to be having a really grand time.

Meanwhile, the bride was still standing in the house with her face covered with that heavy veil. I felt so sorry for her. She sure wasn't enjoying herself like the rest of us.

At some point, the godmother decided it was time to remove the bridal veil. She did it with great ceremony. What a relief it must have been for the bride to get that heavy thing off her head. Finally, she could see, talk, eat and drink something.

A day or two after the wedding cerebration the bride's father-in-law, a brother-in-law or two and the groom's best man went to the bride's house to bring her large chest to the groom's house. The chest was so bulky that it took four men to carry. When they set it down, the bride opened it and distributed her many gifts to the different members of his family, all of whom were gathered around for the occasion.

During the wedding festivities the bride had been unable to talk with anyone until her mother-in-law gave her permission. Thereafter she had to do whatever her mother-in-law said to do. No wonder brides-to-be cried when they left their homes—they must have known what was in store for them. It never occurred to me that someday I might be a bride.

Chapter Fourteen

My Mother's Family

My mother came from a big, well-to-do family, the Arslanians. She had five brothers and three sisters. I heard nothing about my aunts. Each of my five uncles seemed to be quite successful in his pursuit. I was told that one had a fabric store and was himself a tailor; one was the foreman of many workers; one was a merchant who traveled throughout many countries; one had a thriving business of his own; one had gone to a place called Florida in the United States. I was told that the artisans, merchants and bankers in the Ottoman Empire throughout the centuries were mostly Armenians, Jews or Greeks.

We called our uncle *Keri* if he was one of my mother's brothers. An uncle from my father's side of the family was called *hor yekhpayr* which means father's brother.

My mother had told me that her grandfather had been a small person with a long white beard and so devout that sick people would seek him out. It was said that he would lay his hand on the person's head and pray for healing, and their health was restored. After he died people came to his grave site to be healed. They would take the dirt that was on his grave and rub it on their body in hopes of being cured of their maladies. Many came just to sit by his grave to seek guidance.

My mother's father was a well educated, well known and highly respected person who was also a priest. He worked as a mediator and went from province to province to settle disputes. He was taller than most men and quite handsome, even in his black robes. He had the respect of both Armenians and Turks. I remember my mother telling me a story about him that showed what kind of man he was:

"The young son of a very wealthy Turk died suddenly. This Turk was also a high government official. He was in such a state of intense grief that he could not be consoled. Day after day he stayed in a room by himself with his head bowed, not eating or talking. His family asked my grandfather to come to the palatial home of the distraught Turk to help him. He sat with the grieving father for a long period of time, quietly talking to him. Slowly, the Turk lifted his head, was consoled and came back to life. My grandfather was asked to stay on for weeks and was bestowed with many honors."

These honors did not save him or his family from being murdered when the Muslim Turks mandated extermination of all the Armenians.

Chapter Fifteen

My Father's Family

*M*y father's parents' names were Avedis and Nozely Aghjayan. My grandfather was also very well educated for that time and place. He was the town clerk, was an official in a neighboring town before that and had much influence in the province. Written in a book about influential people in this area was the name of Avedis Aghjayan being a long time government official in the town of Uzunlu, which was not far from Burun Kishla. Another book called him a well educated man and in the judiciary system. He was born somewhere between 1855 and 1863.

I had many uncles but the only two I knew and loved as a child were my father's brothers who lived in the village. My father told me about his three younger, bachelor brothers. Yezegiel, the oldest of the three, had been drafted into the Ottoman Turkish army. Melikof and Kegham, the younger brothers, had been living in Ankara before immigrating to the United States.

After Yezigiel had been drafted into the Ottoman Army, he had contacted my grandfather, telling him about the terrible things that were happening to the Armenian soldiers. They were ragged and half starved and were in constant danger of being killed. My grandfather agreed with his son Yezigiel that his two youngest sons should leave the country as soon as it could be arranged. Money was sent to them for their passage and a fresh start in a free country.

As a child, I was not aware of the grim situation that existed. Much later I learned what had taken place in the Ottoman Empire (Turkey) and about the threats my uncles and the rest of the Armenians faced. Armenians lived in fear for a very long time because atrocities and persecutions against Armenians had been going on for countless years. Between 1894 and 1896 over two hundred thousand people of Armenian villages were massacred under the rule and command of Sultan Abdul Hamid.

Henry Morgenthau, the American ambassador to Turkey during the early 1900's, wrote:

> *Had he had his will, he would have massacred the whole nation of Armenians in one hideous orgy in 1895-1896. In 1909 another mass murder of Armenians was carried out by the Turks—thirty thousand were killed. We in Europe and America heard about these events when they had reached monstrous proportions-200,000 Armenians were atrociously put to death. The Sultan found certain obstructions to his scheme, chief of these being England, France and Russia. The satanic plan of destroying a whole race by murder had to be abandoned but the Armenians continued to suffer the slow agony of pitiless persecution.*

After the 1908 Turkish revolution, non-Muslims living in the Ottoman Empire were required to serve in the army. The Balkan Wars of 1911-1913 were the first time non-Muslims fought in the Ottoman army. The Armenian soldiers were not treated as equals and it was a pitiful life to endure. Ragged and nearly starved, they were forced to do back breaking manual labor. Later during the Genocide of 1915, Armenians who were serving in the Ottoman army were disarmed and used for labor battalions and later killed.

Yezagiel, who was drafted in 1911, was sent to Albania to fight and was stationed at a town called Skopje. At this time, Turkey had occupied Greece and the Balkan Countries for decades but was being expelled with the help of France and Britain. Yezegeil, at one battle, was sitting between two Turkish soldiers when an artillery shell burst nearby. The two Turks were swept away but Yezegiel was left without even a scratch. He escaped from the Turkish army but was captured by the British. This turned out to be a fortunate point in his survival in that he was released when the armistice was signed. He stayed in Albania for a while then made his way back to Turkey where he found work, living here and there. In the space of years, he made it to the coastal city of Smyrna. Yezegiel left just a year before the burning of that city and the massacre of the entire Armenian and Greek population by the Turks when the Allies guarding the city suddenly left. He married a young Armenian girl who was living in an orphanage in Smyrna. Together they arrived at Ellis Island on January 21, 1921 aboard the ship Megali Helias.

My uncle Malikof was first to leave the Ottoman Empire. He boarded the ship "Ivernia"in Trieste and was the first Aghjayan to arrive in the United States on June 26, 1912 when he was eighteen. My youngest uncle, Kegham, at the age of seventeen, boarded the ship "La Savoie"at the big harbor town of Le Havre, France. He arrived in the U.S. on March 8, 1914.

Three years after he came, my uncle Kegham left the United States to join a volunteer group of Armenians to assist the European allies in the war effort against Turkey. The United States had, at that time, not yet entered the war. World War I had begun in 1914; America's allies were Russia, England and France fighting against Germany, Austria and Turkey.

The volunteer group was first called "Legion D'Oreient" but became known as the "Legion D'Amenienne." (Armenian Legion). Of the five thousand soldiers in the Legion, twelve hundred were from the United States. Kegham knew that in addition to helping the allies, they would form a force to keep peace in the area when the war was over. This would give him a chance to find out what had happened to his family.

Kegham and the other recruits from the United States were sent to Patterson, New Jersey for the initial training. They embarked from New York City and sailed to Bordeaux, France. This army was to be led by French officers and financed by France to assist the war effort against Turkey.

After receiving their uniforms and weapons in France, the men were shipped to Cyprus for ten months of training and sent to the Palestine front near Jerusalem. Joining British and Australian infantry, they fought valiantly on many battlefields. The Armenian Legion formed the center point of attack on Turkish and German forces at the heights of Arava, just north of Jerusalem. General Allenby had ordered the Armenian Legion to capture the height. The General later said, "I am proud to have the Armenians under my command. They fought brilliantly and had a great part in the victory." In the days to come, the allied armies crushed the Ottoman forces and sent the Turks into full retreat. Turkey surrendered on October 30, 1918 and the war in Europe ended twelve days later with the surrender of Germany.

Kegham, along with many fellow Legionnaires, signed on for two more years and prepared to enter Turkey as peacekeepers. In 1919, the Armenian legion, British and French troops were sent to Cilicia to safeguard the local Armenians, Assyrians and Greeks as they returned to their ancestral homes. The area was in turmoil, with signs of death and destruction everywhere.

What dedication it took for my uncle Kegham to return to Turkey from safe refuge of the United States. He was a brave, compassionate and selfless man. He was also a determined man. He single handedly and against great odds saved my life.

My grandfather must have known that the situation for the Armenians in the Ottoman Empire was intolerable and becoming very dangerous. Why didn't the family flee to another country at an earlier time? Selling his land and livestock to the Turks in that remote area may not have been an option. My grandfather may have found it unbearable to surrender all his land, animals and assets. With the outbreak of World War I in 1914 the Turks closed its borders and did not allow anyone to leave the country. Any attempt to move his large extended family from the mountainous area to another country would have been futile.

The Turks had already taken our camels and horses but we still had the donkeys, the cow, some work animals, our dogs and the sheep. My father and grandfather looked as if they were in pain. I saw tears in their eyes as they held us children close as we awaited our fate. They were told that the village road had been closed. There was no escape. While the crops of fruit and grain were ripening down in the valley and the sheep were grazing in the fields, we were trapped in our village.

Chapter Sixteen

The Terrible Times

The horror began on July 4, 1915 when a young man came to our village with the grim news that the government had mandated that all Armenians living in the Ottoman Empire were to be exterminated. He said Muslim Turkish soldiers and Kurds were going from village to village torturing, raping and killing the Armenians. This brave young man had somehow escaped from his village and was spreading the news so that others would be ready and perhaps protect themselves.

Months before, all Christians had been forced to turn over their guns so there was no means of protection. Although they were not allowed to have guns legally in the Ottoman Empire, a few Armenians had smuggled weapons but there was no chance of survival against the onslaughts. In some places Armenians fought hopelessly until the end.

My grandfather and my father hurriedly gathered together the family gold, jewelry and other valuables, put them in a trunk and buried them in the garden area one night. They made sure that we each knew exactly where it was located. I felt my grandfather's hand on my head as he said, "Maybe one of you will live and will be able to have the valuables and the gold." Perhaps it was better that we children didn't know how grave the situation was.

The following day the Turks murdered the Armenian shepherds who were out with our sheep and threw their bodies in a place for everyone to see.

At the same time, they killed our adult sheep dogs and took the half grown dogs with them.

The real nightmare began on the 10th of July 1915, when our village was surrounded by great numbers of Turkish soldiers and Kurds armed with rifles, axes, knives and other weapons for killing. While my grandmother, my siblings and I hid in a bedroom, soldiers and mercenaries axed the locked door and rushed in. We could hear them attacking my father and grandfather and dragging them out of the house. They searched and emptied the house, taking with them whatever they could carry.

Like ferocious animals, the Turks charged into the church and killed both priests and *Yeretsgeen Mayr*. (Our priest's wife) They took everything of value—all the golden chalices and servers and the handsome rugs. They axed the altar and the crosses.

My grandmother knew the fate that awaited us. Hours before the soldiers came back to our house she put a bottle of poison in my hand and ordered me to give it to my little sister to drink. I was to tell her when my sister had died.

A few hours later the murderers returned to our house and killed my grandmother. We children huddled together in our room with our dead sister.

My father's young wife wasn't killed at this time because she agreed to "marry" one of the Turks. She and the Turk took my two brothers and two sisters with them.

I found out much later what happened to them. The day after he took my sisters and brothers, the Turk told my father's young wife that he was taking them back to our house. Halfway there, he snatched one of my brothers and threw him into a well to drown him. He took the other three children to our empty, ransacked house and left them there with no food or bedding.

One uncle who lived in the village was still alive at the time and lovingly brought them to his house. A short time later the Turks returned to hunt for any Armenian survivors. When they came to my uncle's house, he pleaded for his life and for the lives of the children. He gave the Turks a copper pot full of gold. They took the gold then plunged a knife into his stomach. They threw my surviving brother and two sisters into another well to drown. There wasn't enough water there to drown them quickly. Their cries could be heard for days before they finally died.

It was said that the Turks had tied the hands of the men of our village and dragged them, in groups of thirty or forty, to a place some distance away where there were abandoned mills. They threw scores of the men into these large empty buildings then set fire to them. They boasted that they saved time and bullets this way.

It was also said that my father and grandfather were sadistically tortured and thrown, mortally wounded, into a large pit with others where they suffered a slow, agonizing death.

My father's new wife and the Turk came back to our house later. She showed him where the family treasures were buried. He wasted no time digging them up and together they carried the heavy load to his place. Then the Turk killed her. My family's land, livestock, and house were in the hands of various other Turks, but this one had our gold and valuables—he was now a wealthy man.

The Aghjayan household was no more.

Chapter Seventeen

The Years Of Slavery

I survived because one of the Turkish officers knew my family and perhaps was taken with my red hair. I didn't know what was happening when he picked me up and threw me on his horse. I thought the Turk was going to kill me until he said. "I am taking you to my house. You will be of use to us." Even at age ten, I realized that I was now his property, his slave.

When we arrived, his young wife took one look at me and said, "Why didn't you bring me a bigger girl instead of this little child?" I somehow knew that my life depended on her approval and I pleaded to her to let me stay. I told her I was strong and would work hard to do whatever she wanted me to do; that I knew how to read and write and would teach her children. I talked about taking care of my baby sister and assured her that I would be good to her baby. That did it—she nodded her head and pointed me toward the infant. I called her *hanum* which means mistress in Turkish.

Their house was much like ours but smaller in size with housing for their animals beside them instead of beneath them. While we had a *tunir,* they had a fireplace for the cooking and for heat. They did not have rugs on their bare floors.

Living in the house with the Turkish man was his young wife, two older children by a previous wife, three small children by this wife and also his mother. When I was whipped by the wife, the oldest brother, who was about five years older than me, would try to protect me. He looked after me for some reason.

Shortly after I was brought to the Turkish family, the older sister, who was maybe a year older than I, became very ill one morning and died that night. The grandmother, who was very close to her, was devastated. I don't think anyone knew the reason she died.

It was made clear to me that I was their slave. Soon after I arrived, a woman came to the house with a pouch containing blue dye and needles. She sat me down and ordered me to be still. She took my hand and began sticking needles on the top side. It hurt but I didn't move while she tattooed a bluish circle the size of an American dime. She needled markings within the circle to indicate that I was a slave to this family. Afterward I tried to wash it off but it was there to stay my whole life.

I was not allowed to sleep in the heated room with the family. I slept on the dirt floor in an unheated room, winter and summer. I wrapped myself up in the rags they gave me, but I could not get warm. I could not have survived without their wonderful big dog. She slept right next to me and because of her thick, furry coat I was provided some warmth during the bitter cold nights.

I did not complain or cry. In my thoughts I was home with my beloved family, lying with my brothers and sisters by the warm *tunir* with a thick, soft quilt covering me. I missed them so much and longed to be with them. I was forlorn, but I was not afraid. Just as the shepherd watched over and protected my father's sheep, I felt God's presence shielding me.

One frigid winter day, after coming into the warm house from the cold place where I slept, I went to my *"hanum"* and sweetly asked if I could sleep in the warm room that night to take care of the baby when she awakened during the night. She consented. I took my rags and laid as close to the fireplace as I could and went into a blissful, sound asleep. At daybreak the *hanum* screamed at me and beat me. I had not heard the baby crying during the night. But the main reason for her anger was that I had slept so close to the fire that I had burned my rag bedding. I was never allowed to sleep inside again during the nearly four years I was there.

All the members of this Turkish family had a bad skin condition. In contrast, my cheeks were pink and my skin was clear. The *hanum* would often look at me and say in Turkish, "Ha. You off-spring of a donkey! Look at how healthy you are." Indeed, I was not sick the whole time I was with them.

52

I had no shoes to wear, winter or summer. I had outgrown my shoes and the clothes I wore when I was taken from my home. My *hanum* altered some of her old clothes to fit me but my feet were too small for her old shoes. I would walk out in the snow barefoot.

I was quite small of stature and had a child's body until I was sixteen years old.

I was whipped by the *hanum* and her husband but not severely beaten; I was not molested. The Turkish couple showed consideration in that I was cautioned not to go out to the fields with the farm hands. Visiting Turkish friends of the family would feel sorry for me and express regret as to what had happened. There were many kind Turkish people. I did not understand how some Turks could be murderers while others showed compassion.

I overheard them tell of a Turkish man who had hidden several of my cousins from certain death. The officials found out what he had done. They killed my cousins and put the compassionate man in jail. He soon died there.

Until I was brought to the Turks' house, I didn't know much about cooking. I just enjoyed eating the good meals and snacks that were prepared by my mother and grand mother. Helping the young Turkish wife with all the housework included meal preparation. I had seldom watched my mother and grandmother fix meals but I learned the basics of cooking from the *hanum*. I was surprised and pleased that the food they ate was similar to what we ate. They even had a storage room for food but it was half the size of ours.

Three years went by and one day during the fourth year I was with the Turkish family, a man who said he was my uncle came to their house. I had never seen him before.

It seems that before the massacre my grandfather had approached a kind Turkish family who lived nearby and asked them to be guardians of many of our family possessions. The friendly Turk agreed to store them at his place for survivors to have later. I didn't realize at that time that everyone in my family was dead, but the man who came that day knew.

Apparently, the Turkish friend keeping the family goods would not release them to this man who claimed to be my uncle. Knowing he needed to take some proof of family connection before he could claim my family's things, he had found me. I don't know if he was really an uncle or a just family acquaintance or neither one.

He took me aside and said, "I will to take you back to your village. I am living there now so you can come and live with me." The Turkish man said he would release me if I wanted to go with this man. The other choice was to continue my life as a slave to this Turkish family.

I was nearly fourteen at this time. The decision was mine to make and it had to be made right then. I feared for my life, knowing it was a big risk to go with this strange man. But my heart's desire was to go home. I wanted to find my brothers and sisters and maybe my uncles and cousins. I decided to go.

Within minutes I bid the Turkish family goodbye, hugged their big dog and walked out the door carrying nothing. The man lifted me onto his horse and we quickly left.

When we arrived at our village, I asked that we first stop at my house. The once tidy and substantial structure looked dirty and neglected. I saw many Turks coming in and out the door and noticed the children playing in the dirt outside the house where the garden had been. Many of the houses near ours stood like skeletons of what they once were. Some had tumbled down and those that still stood were occupied by large numbers of Turks and Kurds.

We continued on to the man's living quarters on the edge of the village where I stayed for a few weeks. I learned at that time that my father, my grandparents, my sisters and brothers were all dead, as were both my uncles and their families who lived in the village. I was the only one left.

The indestructible beautiful church, which was the center of all activities and where I had gone to school, stood bleak and ruined. I saw that the floor where once there were precious hand woven rugs was now covered with manure. There were cows housed inside what was once our beloved church. The markers and tombstones in the cemetery were all gone.

The man I was with said that our family's fields, orchards, vineyards, sheep and other animals were in the hands of the Turks and the Kurds. They were tilling our lands and praying to Allah at the appointed hours.

There was nothing left. My dearest family and the familiar surroundings of my happy childhood were no more. I was all alone. I know God wants us to forgive our enemies, but I can never forgive the Muslim Turks.

Chapter Eighteen

Odyssey Begins

$\mathcal{D}$uring the time my uncles Yezegiel and Kegham were in Turkey, they had managed make contact with each other. In talking to many people at different places, Yezegiel found out that his entire family in Burun Kishla was dead except for one niece. He sent word to Kegham. There was no other way but word of mouth to find out about any possible family survivors. My two uncles didn't give up but had continued to ask about their niece everywhere they went. After nearly four years of searching, they found me.

At that time, Yezegiel had a job that involved traveling from place to place so he was able to talk with many different people. Yezegiel managed to find the name and location of the Turkish family who had me with them. He sent the news of my whereabouts to Kegham.

After hearing from Yezegiel, Kegham was anxious to rush things along because he didn't know how long he would remain in Turkey. He was determined to bring me to a safe place in Turkey, then book passage for me to the United States. Many grave obstacles made this undertaking bleak and next to impossible, but he was determined to save me. He stubbornly carried on with his plans for the rescue.

Apparently Kegham had managed to make contact with the Turkish family with whom I had lived and found that I had gone back to the village. He then hurriedly located a Turkish man whose livelihood was smuggling Armenians to safe havens. My uncle Kegham instructed the guide to pick me up in Burun Kishla and bring me to the city of Adana. This city was a long distance south of the village, close to the Mediterranean Sea, where French troops were posted to protect the Armenians and Greeks from the atrocities of the Turks. My uncle was to be waiting for me when I arrived there.

The kind Turk who had my family's belongings had turned them over to the man who claimed to be my uncle. When the man heard that I was going to leave, he began selling the goods. Within a few days he was gone. I was alone in the cold house only a few days before the guide came for me.

There was no need to pack because I had nothing but the clothes I was wearing. Instead of a coat, I had a shawl-like cover for my upper body and a knit hat on my head. On my feet I wore leather pouches.

It was a typical bitterly cold December of 1919 when we started out. We could not wait around for warmer weather because my uncle had told the guide that I must get to Adana as quickly as possible. I had no idea where we were going, how far away it was or how long it was going to take us. Our guide, it turned out, didn't realize how long that journey was going to be either.

There were four of us—an Armenian mother and her young son had joined us. We were on four donkeys, plodding slowly along as fierce wind and snow blew into our faces. It was hard to stay on the pathways because of the dense snowfall. The donkeys slipped many times on the frozen ground but they managed to stay upright and kept up their slow pace.

A raging blizzard was upon us on the second day as we neared Gesaria. There was no way to continue our journey because the freezing snow blew into our faces and bodies and we couldn't see where we were going. Fortunately, this was the city where our guide lived. He took us to his house where we were to stay until the storm was over.

Although Gesaria was only a day's journey from our village in the summer, winter conditions slowed our travel time to two days. The guide was troubled because we had come such a short distance before having to stop.

Each night we made plans to leave the next morning, but the blizzard continued. It felt so good to be in a warm place eating hot food. I was in no hurry to leave. The guide, however, looked troubled and was anxious for us to be on our way. He was afraid that the neighboring Turks would find out that he had three Armenians in his house. His wife gave the woman and me black cloth coverings for our heads so we would look like Turkish women. The guide was especially concerned that my red hair and blue eyes would be too noticeable as we traveled. At his request, I kept my head and face covered and my head lowered for the rest of the journey.

We continued slowly going south in the bitter cold. Within a short time I lost all feeling in my feet and in my hands and I noticed that my skin was now gray in color. My face was also numb. I couldn't stop shivering, as the icy winds cut through my light clothing. At times I felt my father's presence—that I was being carried on his strong shoulders. For a little while I felt warm again.

A deep layer of frozen snow made it hard for the poor donkeys to keep going. They kept losing their footing on the slippery path. The donkeys were also suffering from the biting winds and blowing snow. I thought about our surefooted camels at this time, wishing I was riding on one of them instead of this pitiful, small donkey.

We kept going each day until the sky turned dark and the temperatures dropped even more. The guide found shelter for the night in abandoned houses that were cold and dank. I felt sure these houses once belonged to Armenians who had met the same fate as my family. We had no bedding or hot food. The main purpose of these stops was to feed and rest the donkeys so they could endure the demanding journey the following day.

During the entire journey, the guide was constantly on watch. If the militant Turks found him smuggling Armenians to safety, they would kill him immediately along with the three of us. I remember him as being a very kind man, a good person. He seemed to have compassion for the luckless Armenians. I felt that he was endangering his own life in smuggling us to safety. I trusted him and was not afraid that he would abandon us at any point. I wondered if we were going to run out of money but he assured me there was enough for us to reach our destination.

We stayed at inns a few times where there were warm, clean beds and hot food. At these places I couldn't help but overhear Turks joking and laughing about how many Christian Armenian and Greek they had murdered. They gleefully described their ways of torture and bragged about how many young girls and boys they had mutilated and killed.

Midway in our journey, a Turk stuck out his foot as I was walking out of an inn. He succeeded in tripping me and I fell hard—right on my face.

He laughed as I picked myself up with blood running down from my torn lips and my frost bitten nose. There was no means of treating my injuries. We all got on the donkeys and continued our journey. My lips puffed up and the blood coming from my nose quickly froze on my face. From that point on I was in terrible pain as we continued our journey in the winter cold winds. By this time my fingernails and toenails began falling off my hands and feet.

Later in the journey, we came upon another blizzard. This time the extreme conditions kept us stranded for two weeks in a village where a kind hearted Turkish woman took us into her home.

Along with the malice we had experienced we saw kindness shown to us at this stage of our journey. This wonderful woman fed us well and even took us to a public bath. It felt so good to be clean again and have my hair washed. While we were bathing, another Turkish woman overheard our conversation and knew we were Armenians. Our kind benefactor alerted our guide that this woman was going to tell the Turkish officials about us. Our Turkish guide stopped her as she left the bathhouse and threatened her life if she told anyone about us. She didn't report us immediately but the guide knew she would so we left hurriedly that afternoon.

The most perilous part of our long journey was near its end. This time it took a miracle to bring us through an impossible situation.

We had come to a narrowing in the road and were surprised to encounter Turkish soldiers armed with guns and fierce dogs. They had chosen this particular spot to question and inspect everyone going to Adana. This grim obstacle was most unexpected and our guide knew that there was absolutely no way to get past the soldiers unnoticed. This was the one road to Adana and the only way to get to our destination. In despair the kind Turk lowered his head into his hands and sadly said, "After weeks of travel, this blockage means we can go no further. This is the end for us. We are finished."

A merchant standing nearby saw our dilemma. He told our guide he would be leaving the next morning with his caravan of horses loaded with goods and that we could go through the check point as part of his entourage. Our guide's hopes rose in that we maybe had a chance after all and he heaved a sigh of relief. Later he gave it some thought and a feeling of distrust came over him. He decided against trying to pass through with the merchant.

By this time our guide was desperate. He felt that the only chance we had was to try sneaking through the narrow opening after dark. "We will quietly go past them and hope they will not hear or see us. If our donkeys don't snort or neigh, if their dogs don't attack us or bark, if we can see our way through the narrowing in the dark to get past them, we might make it. If they detect us, we will be killed," said the guide.

The miracle happened. Against all odds, we were able to get through.

Our party was the last to pass that check point and the last group to make it to Adana. Thereafter, Turkish officials closed most of the roads to all travelers trying to get from one city to another, including this one to Adana. Everyone had to stay where they were—travel in Turkey had come to a standstill.

We continued south to a small village called Bozonti, which was near our final destination of Adana. There I saw a train for the first time. In that village there were French soldiers who gave us a hard time in a fun sort of way. They playfully pulled the donkeys' ears and were saying things I didn't understand. I was afraid they were going to unseat me so I got off the donkey. Their smiling faces put me at ease and I knew everything was all right.

Chapter Nineteen

Adana

*I*t was January when we arrived in Adana, a city where French, Turks, Armenians and Greeks lived together and mixed freely. The Armenians and Greeks who had fled the Turkish massacre had come back home, knowing there was protection for them. World War I had ended, the Germans and their Turkish allies had been defeated, and the French soldiers were there keeping peace. The Turks could not carry on with their atrocities while the soldiers were there.

This difficult journey from our village of Burun Kishla to Adana had taken one month. Had it been summer weather, it would have taken only a week to cover this distance.

It was afternoon when we arrived in Adana. Since the guide's job was completed, he bid me farewell and left, as did my fellow travelers. I stood alone, still dressed as a Turkish woman. I was startled when a person walking by snatched off my head covering and said, "You don't need to be afraid anymore."

After being in the freezing weather up to this time, I was jolted by the bright sun and balmy weather. I looked around but stayed where I was hoping my uncle would know I had arrived. In a few minutes, a woman came up to me and said, "Your uncle can not get back here because all the roads have been closed by the Turks. He has managed to travel as far as Izmir." She turned and left before I could say anything or even get a good look at her.

After a short time, I began to feel very ill and feverish and laid down on the ground. I hardly noticed that I was still on the same spot where I had gotten off the donkey and that there were many people walking around me.

I looked up to see an old woman standing beside me. She squatted down and introduced herself as *Digin* Gullian. When she asked, "My child, what are you doing here," I told her of my plight: I knew no one here; I had no food, money or possessions; I spoke only Turkish; I felt very sick; my uncle wasn't here to meet me. This kind woman listened. Stroking my head, she said, "Don't worry. You will feel better soon. There is an orphanage here that will care for you. Come, I will lead you there." I refused to go with her to the orphanage. I knew my uncle would be here soon and I was going to wait for him.

She said no more and left. I must have gone to sleep because I was awakened to *Digin* Gullian's voice saying, "Get up, child. My place is very small but my neighbor will let you stay with her." I slowly rose to my feet and followed her through the narrow streets of Adana. She led me to a little room inside a modest dwelling where I, in my soiled clothes, fell into a wonderful clean bed.

Dear *Digin* Gullian took care of me like a mother. She nursed me, bathed me and fed me all through the six weeks I was very ill and regaining my strength. She brought me condensed milk and bread and later gave me a little money. I survived because of this woman's kindness and loving care.

The neighbors also showed compassion and wanted to help me. One of them told me of the place where I could get free bread. Another neighbor girl, who was a little older than I, made me a wonderful offer. "Come over and let me teach you how to weave rugs. There is a rug-making factory here where you can work. But unless you are experienced, your pay is garnished for five months. You can tell your employer you know how to weave," she said. I eagerly jumped at this wonderful opportunity to learn and to make some money. Within a week I was hired at the rug factory as an experienced weaver.

What a good feeling it was to have a place to stay and some money to spend. A girl named Anahid I met at the rug factory told me how I could earn extra money by spinning wool into thread at home. I jumped at the chance to do that and felt good about it. I had become friends with several other girls working in the factory. We would get together on Sundays and have fun just talking and walking around the city. A few times we hired a carriage with two horses and rode around the countryside. I was learning to speak some Armenian and even a little French. I was not worried that my uncle had not come for me yet.

In the meantime, after months of frustration Uncle Kegham was finally able to reach Adana. The roads were still closed to travelers but he had somehow managed to get through because he was in uniform. Once in Adana, he began searching for me. After talking to many people, he found out from a merchant named Garabed that I was working in the rug factory.

Busily weaving at the rug place one morning, I was startled to see a strange man in military uniform standing before me. He had a big smile on his face when he said "Hello, Maxen." I dropped my head in embarrassment, wondering how he knew my name. The other girls giggled, thinking he must be a suitor who had come to propose marriage. I didn't look at him until he said, "I am your Uncle Kegham" and he embraced me.

I looked up with feelings of great joy and relief. Here, at last, was my uncle. He was looking at me, still smiling, with love in his eyes. I was surprised to see that he didn't look like my father. While my father was tall and fair, Uncle Kegham was shorter with dark hair and warm brown eyes. He was a very handsome man and he looked so young. Later I learned that he was only eight years older than I.

While we were eating our dinner that evening he told me he must leave Adana the next morning but promised that he would to be back as soon as he could. Upon his return we were to leave quickly for France where we would board ship for America. Uncle Kegham gave me what seemed to me an enormous amount of money saying, "We will be going to America soon. You must have some nice clothes made for you." He told me the name and the place of a good tailor who would be expecting me.

My uncle begged me to quit my job and impressed upon me the fact that I should be packed and ready to go when he returned. "We will be leaving Adana immediately because our protection from the Turks will be gone when the French troops pull out," he said. He told me the approximate date he would be coming back for me. Uncle Kegham had inside information that this was going to happen very soon. Why, I wondered, weren't the people in the city told about this so they could prepare to leave also.

The next day I went back to work. I enjoyed being with my friends and didn't want to miss out on the laughter and the friendly chatter. I realized, as morning turned to midday, that what my uncle had asked me to do was urgent and I better do as I was told. I quit my fun job that afternoon.

The next day I walked to the tailor's shop to be fitted for my new clothes. It didn't take him long to make three fine-looking outfits for me. One was a blue silk trimmed in black velvet and the other was a dark red silk with embroidery on the collar and the third was brown trimmed in beige silk. He also made me two slips that were trimmed with lace. I bought underclothes, stockings and high top shoes. I combed my long, red hair away from my face and around so that it hung down in front of my right shoulder. I felt so grown up in my new clothes and hairdo. I was ready to go.

When my uncle returned, he looked approvingly at me and said, "Maxen, you are beautiful. You look like an American." Right before we left, the factory owner came to us and asked if we wanted to buy some rugs to take with us. My uncle said, "No thank you. We can buy better ones in America."

I felt happy and was full of hope. My dear uncle was here and I was going to America with him. I would learn English; I would continue my education—everything was going to be alright.

I was now fifteen years old.

My uncle received word from fellow French soldiers that the troops were leaving Adana the very next day. After a quick dinner we hurriedly left the city that night by horse and carriage.

We traveled to Mersine, a seaport city that was not far, where we could take a small boat to Beirut and on to France from there. There were three other families who left with us that September night.

I heard later that there was mass carnage as the Turks tortured, butchered and burned all the Greeks and Armenians immediately after the French soldiers left. I grieved again, this time for my friends at the rug factory, the kind neighbors, dear Mrs. Gullian and the rest of the innocent Christians who didn't have a chance at the hands of the cruel, barbaric Turks.

Uncle Kegham Aghjayan wearing his Legion D' Armenienne uniform in 1918, with unknown friend.

Chapter Twenty

Ordeals

*W*e had to wait a few days in Mersine until small ship arrived to take us to Beirut, Lebanon. When we reached Beirut, my uncle could not find a place for us to stay. We slept in tents because there were hundreds of other people fleeing just as we were. They were also waiting for the big ship that would take us to France.

We were there a week before we were able to find passage to Marseille, France. We boarded a large and very crowded ship that didn't look very clean to me.

Shortly after we arrived in Marseille, I became desperately ill. I had contacted typhoid fever on the ship. I was delirious with a high fever and soon lost consciousness. The doctors told my uncle I was dying and it was just a matter of time. One doctor told Kegham that there was a chance that I could survive if I regained consciousness.

I awakened, feeling very sick and so weak that I couldn't move my arms or legs. When I opened my eyes, I saw two male nurses standing over me applying ice to my head. I looked down to see that I was naked, sitting in a tub of warm water. I was so embarrassed. Then I saw my uncle who had tears in his eyes because I was conscious and now had a good chance to survive. I was in the hospital for three weeks and my uncle was with me the whole time.

Once again, I had my uncle Kegham to thank for my survival. I know I would have died had I not been in the French hospital receiving the first-rate care they gave me. I believe that they took good care of me because my uncle was in French army uniform. I also believe the French were more learned as to health measures than the rest of Europe at that point in time.

I was discharged when I was able to stand up and to eat solid food. We went to a hotel so I could recuperate and regain my strength. I was "skin and bones" and still very weak. My shiny red hair had fallen out and was replaced by drab, reddish light brown hair. I assured my uncle I would be well and strong very soon.

Uncle Kegham had made all arrangements and had done all the paper work that allowed me to emigrate to the United States. On September 11, 1920, I acquired a French passport, which allowed me to leave France. My passport was also stamped by the consulate of the Republic of Armenia, a short-lived country recognized by the League of Nations to which France belonged. On November 18, 1920 I received a visa from the United States consulate allowing my emigration to the United States.

Uncle Kegham stayed with me for awhile but the time came for him to leave for coastal city of Le Havre to board a ship with his fellow troops for passage to the United States. He reached into a brown leather pouch and handed me the ship's boarding ticket, the train ticket and fifty American dollars. My uncle carefully explained the arrangements he had made for me. He gave me a tight hug, said his good bye and left with a worried look on his face.

Since the families who came with us had gone on, my uncle had found another family who had agreed to wait until I was well, then would accompany me to Cherbourg to board the ship to America. During the time I was gaining strength I became good friends with an Armenian girl who lived in Marseille. She was fun to be with and she enjoyed teaching me more of the French and Armenian languages. By time I left, we were talking to each other in French.

It was several weeks before I was strong enough to take the train to Cherbourg. When the time came to leave, I packed my things in a hurry and we were on our way to the train station.

It was the first time I had been on a train and I was very excited. It took nearly two days to make the journey from Marseille to Cherbourg. All I could think of was that I would soon be in the land called America. What a wonderful adventure I was having.

From the train station in Cherbourg we, along with many others, were transported to the dock area by horse and buggy. I saw that small boats were taking people to the big ship that was anchored a good distance away from the dock. For some reason, we were boarding in the evening. There was a big mass of people waiting to board, talking and shouting in many different languages. People were pushing and shoving in their effort to get into the small boats that took passengers to the big ship.

I hung back and waited until the very last to board. Just as I was about to step into the small transport boat I happened to see a big basket someone had left behind. It was filled with wonderful things to eat—chocolates, apples, pears, cheeses and crackers. I grabbed the food basket in one hand and my suitcase in the other hand and jumped into the boat and onto the massive ship.

Chapter Twenty One

The Voyage

This gigantic steel ship with its two funnels and four masts was called the Zeeland of the Red Star Line. We set sail that night of December 3, 1920.

The British ship launched in 1900, was 561 feet long and 60 feet wide and had accommodations for over a thousand people. The six hundred of us who were steerage (third class) passengers did not mingle with the three hundred who had first class accommodations. They were on another deck with their own dining room and spacious cabins.

In the steerage class section of the boat, men and women were separated to different parts of the ship. The sleeping areas were solid masses of bunks, six high along the sides of the boat. I climbed up a tall ladder to the very top bunk and managed to take the food basket with me. I enjoyed every bit of the delicious treats during the voyage, especially chocolates that I had been introduced to in France.

There was a bed check each night to see that the men and women were in their separate sections. I noticed a man sneak into our area so that he could sleep with his wife. When they were checking us out that night, my giggling attracted attention and they found the man who was in his wife's bunk. Although he protested, he was quickly sent back to the men's quarters.

When we were out to sea, a great many of the passengers became seasick but I felt fine and took care of those who needed help. At dinner time only a few people showed up. A boy about my age and I were there for all the meals. One time he tried to kiss me and I hit him in the face with my hat.

On the ship I was both excited and uneasy because I didn't know what awaited me in my new world. I was a little anxious because I didn't know how to speak the language spoken in America. How would I communicate? Then my thoughts would turn to my dear Uncle Kegham and I felt happiness again. He would be waiting for me when I walked off the ship. I was eager to meet my other two uncles.

It took eleven days to cross the Atlantic to the United States. There were times during the trip that I would see the faces of my mother, father and those of my sisters and brothers as I looked out at the gray sea. Doubts, fears and sadness came back to haunt me for a little while. However, deep in my heart I knew that God had helped me all through the terrible times and He was with me now and always.

On December 14, 1920 we reached the United States of America.

Chapter Twenty Two

Ellis Island

I was full of excitement as I walked off the ship at Ellis Island with my ship acquaintances. This Immigrant Station in New York had opened in 1892, twenty eight years before I arrived. I was one of the twenty million immigrants who passed through its doors to begin a new life in America.

All of the immigrants who came on the big ship, Zeeland, were put in a huge space where everyone was to stay until relatives came to claim them. I stayed close to the Balakian family who had come with me from Marseille. I was a little uneasy but not at all worried.

Later I became thirsty and went to the fountain for a drink of water. When I returned the Balakians were gone! Gradually almost everyone else left as their names were called on the loud speaker. I stood anxiously listening, waiting for my name to be called. Hours passed and it was night time when I became alarmed. I realized that I could be sent back to France or Turkey if no one came for me.

A boy who looked a little older than I was came over and patted me on the shoulder and said, "Don't cry—someone will come for you. I have been here waiting for three weeks." Three weeks? That was not a comforting thought but I was confident that my uncle Kegham would come soon.

Someone brought me an evening meal and I slept in the same big room in a bunk bed that night. Just as I awakened the next morning I heard my name being called on the speaker. What a great relief it was when I saw my uncle's handsome, smiling face.

Chapter Twenty Three

Roslindale

*A*s we traveled to Boston and onto its suburb of Roslindale I was startled when I saw a black man for the first time. As a child I had heard that they were black because they came out of the ground. I was fascinated with everything I saw: the tall buildings and the store fronts, the different kinds of people walking the streets and the way they were dressed, the sights and sounds of my new country.

We finally came to the boarding house where both my two uncles were staying. There, I saw my Uncle Malikof for the first time. I would have known him anywhere because he looked so much like Uncle Kegham. My oldest uncle Yezegiel and his new wife would also be arriving in a few weeks.

An older Armenian couple, named Helen and Garo, owned the boarding house. When Helen saw me come in, she hugged me and announced, "God has sent me a beautiful daughter." She welcomed me in her loving, gentle manner and saw to my comfort. For the first time since becoming an orphan, I felt the warmth of a caring family. It felt good.

Helen had been a teacher and we talked about where I would do my schooling. She and her kind-faced husband, Garo, said they longed for a daughter like me and would take care of all my needs if my uncles would let them.

Helen told me that more and more American women were educating themselves and earning a living. She explained Women's Suffrage. That very year the 19th amendment had been ratified, giving women the right to vote. It made them equal with men in political matters, she said. I looked at her puzzled, not knowing what she was talking about. That's when she realized that I knew nothing about the democratic form of government where people actually choose their leaders. She patiently explained American politics and democracy to me.

I shared my dream with her: of going to school and becoming a teacher. The fact that I knew no English didn't bother me now—I knew I could quickly learn the language. Helen understood my determination and assured me that she would help me achieve my goal.

How wonderful it was to be in a free land with loving people. How elated I was with this wonderful new phase of my life which would include continuing my education that had been cut short when I was ten.

My oldest uncle, Yezegiel and his young bride arrived five weeks after I did. While I was happily thinking about my future, my uncles were arranging a marriage for me. I was not yet sixteen years old.

For three months I was in high spirits. I didn't know that my future had already been decided upon by my uncles while I was still in France.

It seems that my Uncles Malikof and Kegham had become friends with a man called Armen Caragozian while they were all teenagers living in Ankara, Turkey. He had also immigrated to Boston where he had worked for awhile in a candy store and had later moved to the San Joaquin Valley in Central California. When Malikof received word from Kegham that I was alive and that I would soon be coming to the United States, he had written to Armen and offered me as his bride.

One day in late March, my three uncles asked me to sit down with them so they could tell me about their plans concerning my future. I waited in happy anticipation of their being in agreement with my staying with Helen. The smile left my face as I listened to what Yezegiel was saying. He, being the oldest surviving male in the Aghjayan family, was now the spokesman and the decision maker. He told me that I was to be married very soon.

Yezegiel informed me that Malikof and Kegham had a fine friend named Armen Caragozian who would be a good husband for me; he had a grocery store in a place called Parlier, California; he and the Aghjayans were from the same province in Turkey; he was ten years my senior; he was a hard worker and an honest man and he had agreed to take me as his wife.

I couldn't believe what I was hearing. I had just arrived—why were they in such a hurry to marry me off? They knew I wanted to stay with Helen so I could continue with my schooling. Weren't things different in this new country? Why didn't they talk it over with me instead of ordering me to marry this man? I had not given marriage a thought.

I cried and turned to my beloved uncle Kegham, hoping he would say something on my behalf. He looked away from me and kept silent. I put my head down in great sadness, knowing the marriage plans for me were in place and the decision was final.

My optimism and happiness were short lived. I loved my uncles but I never could understand why they did this, and I found it hard to forgive them.

Maxen's passport picture taken in France. at the age of fifteen. Date-1920.

Armen Caragozian and Kegham Aghjayan, young bachelors in 1912.

Maxen's uncles Melikof and Kegham as young men. Date unknown.

Maxen's oldest uncle Yezegeil. Passport picture dated 1920.

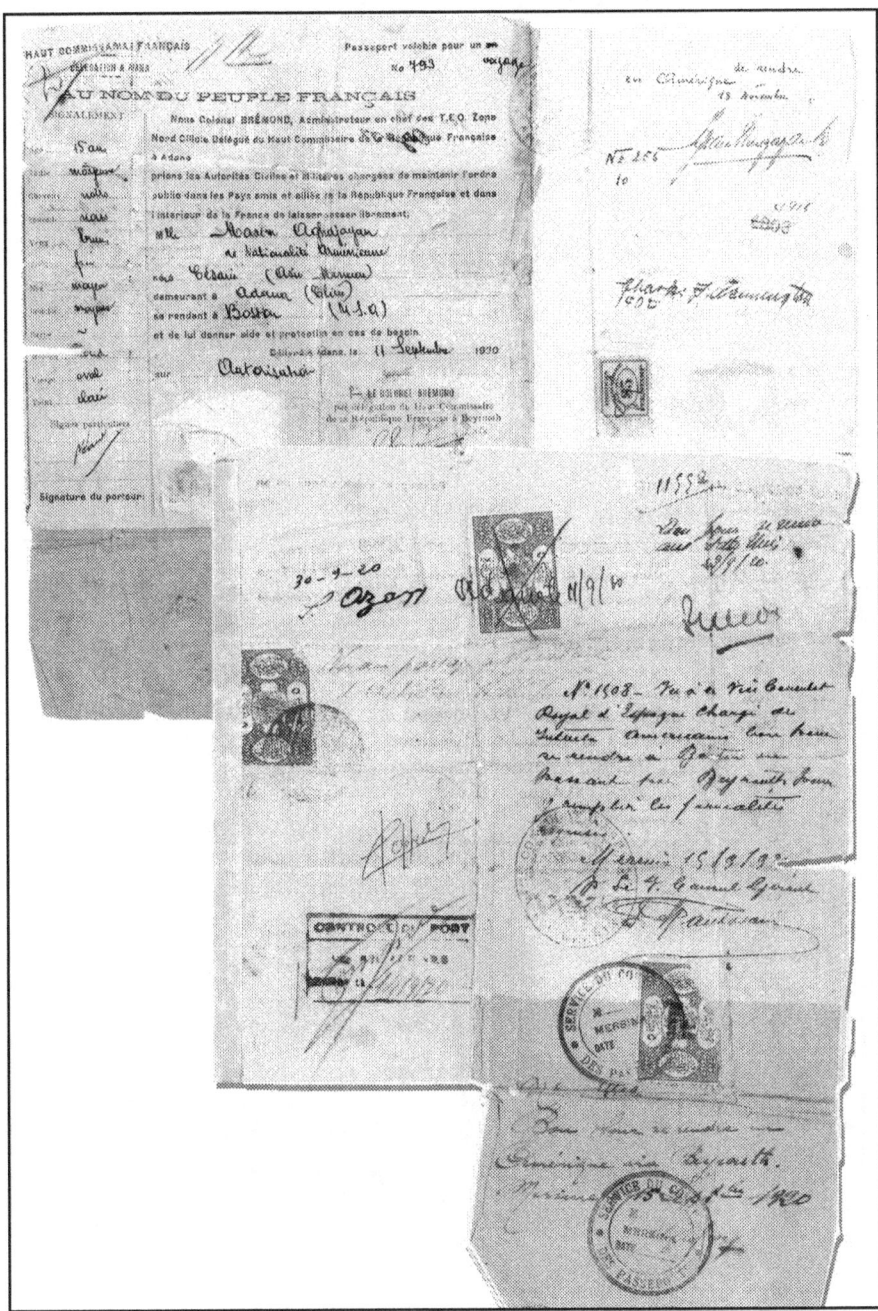

Maxen's passport to the United States.

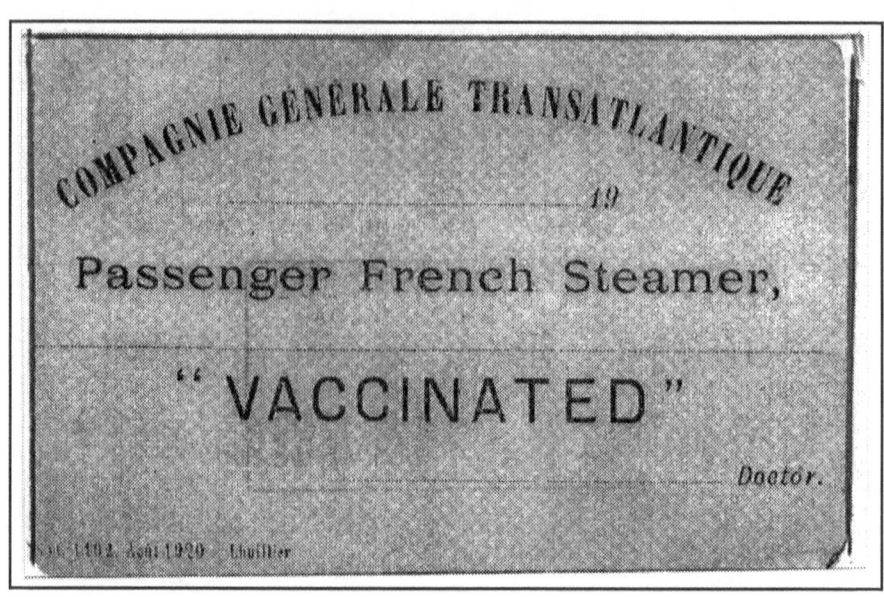

Maxen's ship document bearing proof that she had been vaccinated for smallpox. At Ellis Island this card was pinned to her coat in a prominent place.

Cette carte doit être conservée pour éviter une détention à la Quarantaine comme sur les chemins de fer des États-Unis.

Diese Karte muss aufbewahrt werden, um Aufenthalt an der Quarantäne, sowie auf den Eisenbahnen der Vereinigten Staaten zu vermeiden.

Conservate questo biglietto onde evitare detenzione alla Quarantina e sulle Ferrovie degli Stati Uniti.

A written document instructed Maxen and fellow passengers to keep this card to avoid detention at Quarantine, both here and on railroads in the United States.

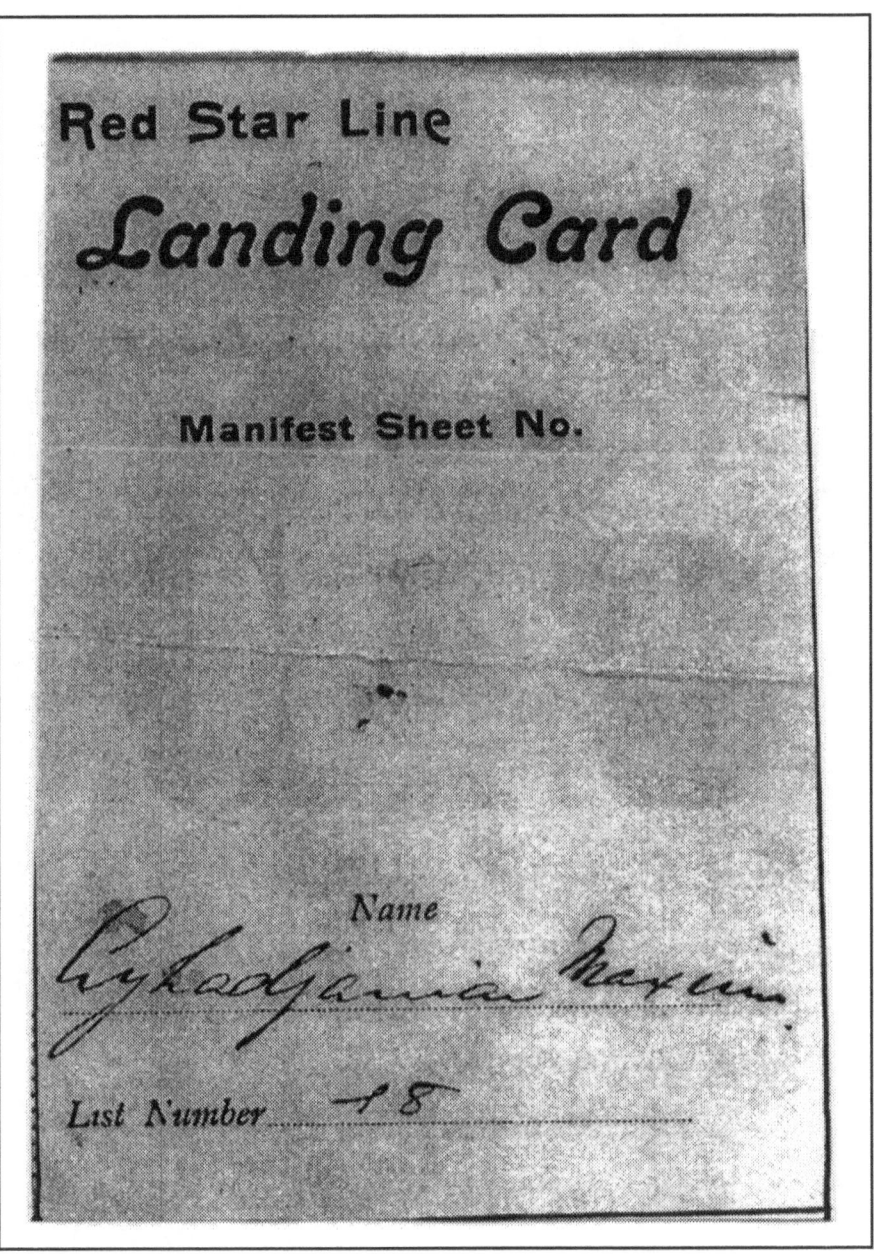

Maxen's ship landing card. Her first and last names were misspelled on both the landing and inspection card.

Red Star Line

Inspection Card

Current No.

(Immigrants and Steerage Passengers.)

752

Name of ship,

from Cherbourg   *-3 DEC 1920*

Name of Immigrant,   *Aghadjianian Maxim.*

Last residence,   *Cesarea Adana*

Inspected and passed at Cherbourg

	Passed at quarantine, port of	Passed by Immigration Bureau,
	U. S.	port of
	(Date)	(Date)

(The following to be filled in by ship's surgeon or agent prior to or after embarkation.)

Ship's list or manifest,   *18*   No. on ship's list or manifest,

Berth No	Steamship inspection	1st day	2	3	4	5	6	7	8	9	10	11	12	13	14	to be punched by ship's surgeon at daily inspection

No immigrant boarded the ship without inspection card.

Part Two

Remembering Maxen

Chapter Twenty Four

Westward Journey

*O*nce again, Maxen was sitting in a train, looking out the window at unfamiliar scenery. Four months before, she had taken her very first train ride from Marseille, France, to the port city of Cherbourg where she boarded ship for America. She had been excited and happy as she anticipated the adventures that awaited her during the ocean voyage and the wonderful life she would have in a new land.

She was in America now but this was a journey that was filled with dread and apprehension. Uncle Yezigiel and his new wife Ramella were accompanying her from Boston to Central California. Within a short time Maxen was to be married to Armen Caragozian, a man she had never seen before. Her cheerfulness had vanished and although the three of them were sitting together, there was very little conversation.

Cross-country train travel in the early 1920s was slow and tedious, but that suited Maxen. She was in no hurry to get to California. Trains were the only means of cross country travel at that time—going by plane or car was not a real possibility in 1921. There were few paved highways as yet and airplanes were still in their infant phase.

As Maxen looked around at the others on the train, she felt out of place in her finely tailored silk dress. She noticed that the other female passengers were simply dressed in cotton dresses or casual light weight suits. Maxen vowed she would do away with her European-looking clothes as quickly as she could and dress in a more casual manner like the American girls.

Maxen, Yezegiel and Ramella arrived in Fresno, California on May 8, 1921. Armen was to meet them there and bring them the twenty miles or so to Parlier, where Armen had settled. They didn't know what Armen looked like but there was no problem with identifying him at the train depot.

From the train window Maxen saw a stocky young man pacing as he eagerly looked at each person getting off the train. He was neatly dressed in Levis and a white shirt. His thick mass of dark hair was combed over to one side and under the thick black eye brows were brown eyes gleaming with anticipation. In his hands he carried a gold-tone metal box. When Armen saw the three of them step off the train he knew at once who they were. His face became one big smile when he gazed at the well dressed, petite girl, the last person to step off the train. He had not expected a bride this young and beautiful. He handed Maxen a gilded box, which was filled with store-bought chocolates.

Maxen was not smiling. Her bright blue eyes grew a shade darker with anxiety. Her face held the same look it had had nearly six years before when the Turk took her to his house as a slave. Once again she was being forced into a life changing situation beyond her control—this time it was marriage.

Maxen knew very well that arranged marriages were customary in the Old Country. But she was certain that her father would not have chosen this man because their family backgrounds were quite different. Hers was a prominent, educated family while Armen came from a peasant family.

The distress Maxen felt was two-fold: she was being forced into this marriage; she could not continue her education. She visualized her father's earnest face during the times he had promised her she would go to the American college in Gesaria. He was gone, but her desire for learning had not died.

Inside Maxen's suitcase were two burgundy red books, bound and printed in Constantinople (Istanbul). One was an English-Armenian Practical Dictionary printed in 1905 and the other was an Armenian-English Practical Dictionary printed in 1910. Maxen had them with her when she boarded ship in France. She was immersed in both books on the train ride to California and had begun her studying on the long voyage to America so she would know a few words of English.

As she stood on the train platform looking at Armen, her first thought was that she did not want to be a wife—she knew nothing about men or being married. Various other thoughts raced through her mind, but she kept her silence and accepted the fact that whatever she did or said at this point would make no difference. This was to be her destiny.

In his pocket Armen had a ring, a small sparkling diamond set in a tiffany gold setting. Before they left the train depot, he solemnly placed it on her finger, making the engagement official. Her uncle and Armen were already talking about the wedding plans as they picked up the suitcases. Yezegiel was now the oldest male of the Aghjayan family, the patriarch. He considered it his responsibility to see that his niece had a good husband and a proper wedding.

Chapter Twenty Five

The Wedding

On the morning of May 22, 1921, Maxen was helped into an ankle length, white chiffon wedding dress. The bridal attire was complete with an attractive veil, white high heeled shoes, elbow length gloves and an elaborate bouquet.

The wedding took place in Parlier at the farm home of Armen's good friends, the Avazians. Making the twenty mile trip from the Armenian Apostolic Church in Fresno, Reverend D. Markarian performed the ceremony at 10:20 A.M. He recited the full marriage rites which lasted a full hour. Toward the end of the ceremony Maxen's anxiety was heightened when her veil caught on fire from a nearby candle.

The photographer was there, ready with his black breadbox-size camera, sturdy tripod and a suitable backdrop. He also had a well-worn wedding veil Maxen could borrow for the picture. A pleased twenty-six year old groom dressed in a handsome suit and his unhappy sixteen year old bride posed for a solemn wedding portrait.

The wedding license listed Maxen as eighteen years old because, at her actual sixteen, she was too young to marry legally.

After the wedding ceremony, Maxen remembered chicken and rice pilaf being served for lunch and a small wedding cake with coffee afterwards. It was a small affair, not the two day celebration with music, dancing, feasting and merriment as weddings were in her happy childhood days. Another old world custom that had gone on for centuries was now a thing of the past. It was a new country and a different way of living.

"At least I don't have to stand up for hours with a thick veil covering my face like the Old Country brides", she thought, "and I won't have a mother-in-law telling me what to do." That reflection and the fact she was among genteel, kind people comforted her somewhat, and she was less frightened.

Wedding portrait of Maxen and Armen on May 22. 1921.
Maxen, age 16. Armen, age 26.

Maxen and Armen's marriage license. Her age was written as eighteen but she was only sixteen at the time.

Marriage License
and Certificate

20900

and

Filed for Record and Recorded
at Request of

Rev. D Markarian

this _24_ day
of _May_ A. D. 19 21
at _20_ min. past _10_
o'clock _A. M._, and Recorded in Book
Official Records
_102_ of Marriage Certificates,
on Page _157_ Records of
Fresno County.

R. N. Barstow
County Recorder.

By
Deputy Recorder.

Armin Gregosian
P.O. Box 9, Parlier, Calif.

Front side of marriage license,

Chapter Twenty Six

San Joaquin Valley

*P*arlier was one of many bustling small towns located in the middle of the fertile farm lands in the San Joaquin Valley of central California. The towns were within a few miles of each another with acres of farmland separating them. There were all situated near the western foot of the magnificent Sierra Nevada. This massive wall of mountains, more than four hundred miles long and about seventy miles wide, runs up and down east-central California. Three splendid National Parks are nearby: Kings Canyon, Sequoia and Yosemite. Kings Canyon National Park, at 6500 feet in elevation; the home of the majestic and ancient Giant Sequoia, is located less than forty miles from Parlier.

It didn't take Maxen long to become aware of the mountain range which rimed the valley. As she gazed at the fertile land covered with rows and rows of vigorous grapevines and orchards of fruit trees, she found comfort. This place was so much like her beloved homeland. "The only difference is," she thought, "I will be living in the valley instead of the mountains." It was still pleasantly cool when she arrived in May. She was soon to find out that the hot summer temperatures were the same as in her homeland valley.

Newcomers burned the soles of their feet if they foolishly went barefoot in the summer. Temperatures in the San Joaquin Valley were in the high nineties and often over a hundred degrees. Sometimes, a light breeze stirred the dry hot air a little during the day and made the nights more tolerable. From May through October there was little or no rain, which provided a long growing season and gave the farmers time to dry the various fruits, such as grapes, apricots, peaches and nectarines.

The nearby Sierra Nevada was the lifeline of the hot, dry valley. Water from the melted snow flowed into rivers, was dammed in reservoirs, and funneled into wide canals to the farms below, where vast acres of trees, grapevines and other crops waited to be watered.

Farming was the very backbone of the San Joaquin Valley. Maxen noticed and found it odd that most Californians called their farms *ranches* no matter what they grew on the land.

Chapter Twenty Seven

The Immigrants

𝒯wenty-six million people came to the United States between 1865 and 1915. The population of Parlier, and all the San Joaquin Valley, was typical—new immigrants and descendents of earlier settlers.

Most of the immigrants, including Maxen and Armen, came with little more than faith and hope to a country where they could better themselves. Some arrived with only a tattered suitcase in hand. They found what they had searched for—a democracy, a land free of oppression. This was a place where they could work, gain an education and, given the opportunity, prosper. Facing challenges and severe hardships with courage and resourcefulness, they neither expected nor did they receive any handouts.

Many of the San Joaquin Valley's immigrants were Armenians from what was then the Ottoman Empire. (Now Turkey) Hagop Seropian, the first Armenian who came to Fresno in 1881, found a climate similar to his homeland and wrote to others about the fertile valley. As a result, numbers of Armenians came to this area—agriculture was their forte. Many developed new kinds of agricultural products. The Seropians were the innovators, packaging and shipping dried fruits. The Markarians showed how figs could be produced and marketed profitably. The Arakelian family began the growing of cantaloupe and watermelon when they imported several types of melons that grew well in California. Other Armenians brought in new varieties of grapes that thrived in the West. The Setrakian family started the large-scale marketing of raisins. Numerous other

Armenians planted and operated large scale farms of vegetables, fruits and nuts, mainly almonds and walnuts.

The largest number of Armenians came to the United States between 1900 and the beginning of World War I in 1914. They settled mostly in the Northeast with a number of them moving west to California, Washington and Oregon. The immigrants arriving in the teens had a more difficult struggle because time had taken a grim downturn, and dismal conditions persisted for nearly two decades in the agricultural areas.

Chapter Twenty Eight

Misfortunes

It was the Roaring Twenties and prosperity for the nation as a whole, but tough times for the farmers throughout the country. During the 1920's, when the rest of the nation was on a joy ride, the U.S. farmers were barely surviving.

At the time of their marriage in 1921, Armen had been in America for eight years and had a small grocery store. He had toiled at many jobs, which included working at a candy factory in Watertown, Massachusetts and being a dishwasher in Fresno. He had eventually accumulated the money needed to start a grocery store. Armen had a mind for mathematics, which came in good stead in tallying the bills for the customers. He also had a generous heart and extended credit to other immigrants who patronized his store, many of whom were farmers and his friends and neighbors. When they were unable to pay their tabs, the store went under.

Armen began farming full time after losing the grocery store. He worked near Parlier as a tenant farmer on a ranch that belonged to M.M. and Rachel Davidian. Maxen and Armen lived on the Davidian ranch in a tank house, which resembled a short, squatty light house with a big water tank perched high on top. The small living quarters was on ground level. This cramped space was their home during the many difficult years of the 1920s.

By 1927, Armen and Maxen had managed to save $800.00. They bought a sixteen acre ranch, which included 2000 raisin trays and seventy "sweat boxes" (For drying and storing grapes, apricots, nectarines, and peaches), from the Davidian's. This ranch was nearby, between Reedley and Parlier. Armen and Maxen agreed to pay $7,200 for this small ranch, the $800 cash down, and half of each year's crop to pay the $6,400 balance due in annual installments on each December 1, at seven percent interest.

Armen and Maxen worked to exhaustion on the ranch, day after day, month after month, year after year, but they still fell behind in their payments. As crop prices continued to drop, the ranch failed to generate enough money to pay the mortgage and buy food, clothing and bare necessities for the Caragozian family. Indeed, the ranch could not always feed Maxen, Armen and their two children. Son John recalled that, as a young boy, he suffered from hunger at times. Maxen and Armen failed to make the full payment on December 1, 1933. The following month, in January, 1934, the Davidian's lawyer sent Armen written notice, giving him twenty-four hours to reach agreement with the Davidians or face legal action. Apparently, some agreement was reached, as the Caragozians continued to own the ranch at least through December 1, 1934 when they paid the Davidians $284.03 in interest and $195.23 in principal.

Eventually, however, Armen and Maxen lost their ownership of this ranch. Son John recalled it as a tragedy: "Mom and Pop worked so very hard, but they ended up with so little." The Caragozians continued as tenants, barely eking out a living, and trying to save to buy another ranch.

Chapter Twenty Nine

Motherhood And Grief

*M*axen and Armen's first child was a daughter, who was born on March 6, 1922. She was named Mary for Maxen's mother, Mariam. It was said that she was a beautiful and extremely intelligent girl; a joy to her parents. She started first grade speaking only Armenian but was an eager, quick learner and was advanced to the third grade the following year.

Their second child was John Leo. Levon was the name of one of Maxen's brothers, and the English equivalent Leo was on the birth certificate but on his December 25, 1926 baptism his first name was John, after a family friend, and Leo became his middle name. John was born on September 27, 1926 and was very ill as an infant but recovered. Under Old Country values, he had special status as a boy. John was an intelligent but mischievous child. Once, in 1932 when Maxen was trying to crank the old Model T, he playfully pushed down the spark lever inside the car causing the crank to turn counter clock-wise which caused a break to his mother's arm in two places. He thought it was fun to sometimes let the air out of the tires when company came to visit. John, like his siblings, had an over-abundance of vitality.

In the summer of 1930, their first born child Mary was climbing a fig tree while playing with two friends when she fell, rupturing a kidney. She suffered great pain from the resulting infection. Although Dr. Fleming, a Scottish bacteriologist, had discovered penicillin in 1928, it was not yet available for public use. The only cure was to remove the kidney, which could be successfully done at that time. Sadly, Maxen and Armen did whatever they could within their financial limits but did not have the money to take her to San Francisco for the surgery. After weeks of suffering, Mary died on July 2, 1930, at the age of eight.

Mary's suffering and death caused deep, wrenching sadness for Maxen, Armen and John. John recalled how abandoned he felt: his father driving the Model T, his mother sitting next to him cradling Mary as they went back and forth between the ranch and the local doctor. Both parents were thinking about no one other than their dying daughter, with four-year-old John sitting all alone, feeling forsaken, in the back seat.

The ever present sorrow was sometimes unbearable but Maxen's incredible strength and unshakable faith made it possible for her to cope. Until the end of her life, Maxen felt the pain of losing her beautiful first-born. Armen's intense grief made it impossible for him to go about his tasks, thus leaving the farm work undone.

Maxen and Armen could not afford to pay for their daughter's funeral when she died in 1930. Their good friends, Enoch and Mary Kashishian loaned them fifty dollars for the burial. The Kashishian's daughter Quinn recalled that the entire community was traumatized by Mary's death. Parents would not allow their children to climb trees for a very long time.

When Maxen sent word to her two uncles Melikof and Kegham about the tragedy and about Armen's grief- stricken condition, they did not hesitate in taking action. They quickly made all the necessary arrangements to be gone for an indefinite period of time. The two uncles left Roslindale, Massachusetts in a 1929 Whippet car, traveling slowly over terrible roads and across rough terrain in their journey to California. They finally made it to Maxen and Armen's small residence, bringing them both support and solace. Toiling in the vineyards through the blistering summer heat, Melikof and Kergham tended the fields. Although they were merchants and had never farmed before, they quickly learned how to plow the fields, irrigate, and did whatever else was necessary. They continued working through the autumn harvest of the grapes and left only when they were sure that Armen was going to be alright. Encouraging Maxen and Armen the best they could, they said their goodbyes and began their long, tough cross-country trip home. Maxen knew that her dear uncles had shown their devotion to her and Armen with this sacrificial journey and labor of love.

Two years following the death of their adored first born, Maxen and Armen were blessed with another baby daughter they also named Mary. The baby barely survived a difficult birth. A severe intestinal illness ensued and she was close to death twice before she was a year old. Later this child caused them more anxiety because she liked to climb high up into trees, the water tower or the hay loft because she thought it was great fun to jump off. Twice they rushed her to the doctor for sutures. They were relieved when she grew older and lost interest in this activity.

Maxen's last child was born eight years later. The pretty fair-haired baby girl was named Helene, after the caring landlady in Roslindale, Massachusetts, who had loved Maxen as a daughter.

Maxen and Armen with firstborn daughter Mary. Date 1924

Kegham, Armen and Melikof in the vineyard.
Boy unknown. Date- 1930

Family portrait of Maxen and Armen with their first born daughter, Mary and their son, John. Date 1928

Family portrait of Maxen and Armen with son John and second daughter
Mary. Date- 1938

Maxen, Armen, John, Mary and Helene plus the faithful family dog, Laddie in the autumn of 1944.

Front side of Caragozian ranch home

The house in the middle of vineyards, with the walnut
tree towering on the back side.

Chapter Thirty

The Great Depression

*I*n 1929 the greatest calamity since the Civil War hit the United States. The great American Depression was felt all over the world—European countries had depended on the American dollar in the way of exports, tourism and loans. Foreign trade collapsed and agricultural prices in California hit a new low.

In California and elsewhere many farmers, who were already struggling, lost out completely. Crop prices were so low that often the crops would not even be harvested. One year the selling price for a ton (Two thousand pounds) of the raisins was eight dollars and a ton of fresh grapes sold for two dollars. The Caragozians and other ranchers left their grapes on the vines and the prime fruit in the orchards fell to the ground and rotted. Those who earned their livelihood working on farms had no jobs. Farms were being sold at rock bottom prices. Poverty was the norm and many families went hungry. Banks were not willing to lend money to the farmers. During one parade in Parlier, son John recalled horses pulling a farm wagon loaded with raisins, topped by a sign, "For Sale, But No One Will Buy."

There was no welfare, no food stamps, no Medicaid, no soup kitchens, no handouts—there was nowhere to turn for help. It was sink or swim in the twenties and the early thirties for the nation's farmers.

Some of the northeastern states were less affected because they had new industries that were producing cars, aircraft and radios. With the exception of some Southern states, the rest of the nation felt the human suffering, in the way of near starvation, abject poverty and pessimism. In the Great Plains, from Canada to Texas, acres of crops were ruined by two years of drought and catastrophic dust storms that left the land a barren wasteland. There was an exodus to California by many of these farming families, their meager belongings tied to the top of their cars. Most of these destitute families came from Oklahoma and Arkansas and were labeled Okies and Arkies by the Californians, as chronicled by John Steinbeck in the <u>Grapes of Wrath</u>. In other areas 3,000,000 factory workers were without jobs, hundreds of thousands of families roamed the land throughout the nation in search of work and sustenance.

Many of the Armenian immigrants were oblivious to the national trends. Indeed, many immigrants knew little beyond their own locales. Son John recalled a neighbor, an old Armenian farmer, who liked to learn English words from John. One day the old farmer motioned for John to come over. The farmer began complaining (in Armenian): "I just can't learn this English language. I talk to the Americans in town, I listen to the radio, I even go to night school, and I just can't learn the language. But what really bothers me is that the Okies come here and learn the language, just like that."

Chapter Thirty One

The New Ranch

*D*espite their poverty, Armen and Maxen were better off than some of their friends. In 1931, Armen lent $500 to a fellow farmer Digran Panosian. Armen's and Maxen's generosity even extended to bringing Panosian home cooked meals. Armen also lent lesser sums to other needy friends at various times.

Finally, Maxen emphatically told Armen, "If there is money for lending to our friends, there must be enough to put a down payment on some land!" Soon after accumulating $1000 for the down payment, they bought another ranch for the purchase price of $3000 on January 23, 1936. The twenty acre ranch was only a mile or so from where they had been living.

A wide irrigation canal was the boundary line on two sides of their new place. The landmark at the ranch entrance was a large, very old cottonwood tree that stood on the canal bank A few yards from the tree was a narrow rickety wooden bridge that led to the dirt driveway. The bridge, which was nothing more than long slabs of wood nailed down to base timbers, spanned the eighteen foot width of the irrigation canal. It had no railings and was just wide enough for a single car to creep across. Those coming over the Caragozian bridge did so very slowly and cautiously, especially at night, knowing there were only inches to spare between them and the deep, swiftly flowing water beneath.

Son John recalled the new ranch as having been neglected by its previous owners. The vineyard was forty-five years old, and weeds proliferated.

Also the land was covered with tall Eucalyptus trees that were as big as three feet in diameter. Slowly but surely, down came the trees and up went a neat two bedroom white farmhouse that sported a dark green roof. The family happily moved into their new home and breathed in the good smell of new wood. Next on the scene was a big barn that was painted light gray. It was a large structure that housed the horses and cow on one end, the farm equipment on the other end and the many bails of hay in the wide middle space. The land was tilled and the first new grape vines were planted in the fertile ground. .

In time, the Thompson seedless grapes and Muscat grapes were picked and were dried into raisins and a working ranch was created. Armen continued to work both on his land and as a tenant farmer for the Davidian's until the new ranch could support the family. Maxen worked on the farm and helped mastermind many of the needed improvements. Armen begrudgingly observed but would not admit that her suggestions were sound and practical.

Chapter Thirty Two

The Way It Was

Life on the Caragozian family ranches was, through the early 1930s, one of ongoing poverty. Thoughts of her comfortable, carefree childhood with her loving family must have entered Maxen's mind, but she rejected negative thoughts and self pity. Even by standards of the time, the ranch was just average. In fact, not even all of the acreage could be farmed. Land had to be set aside for alfalfa to feed the mules and the cow which produced milk, so the family could have home-made butter, yogurt and cheese. Additional land was used for the barn, a chicken coop, the vegetable garden and Maxen's flower garden.

For Maxen, flowers were a necessity—the essence of civilized living. She was frugal and resourceful in every way, with bountiful flowers being her only small luxury. Surrounding the farmhouse were bright, sweet-scented flowers, bright green ferns and multi-hued lilacs grew alongside the front lawn. Big, robust hydrangea bushes, sporting soft pink blooms, were silhouetted against the white siding of the house. Leaning against the sunny side of the barn were fragrant sweet peas that grew six feet tall. There was a flower, plant or bush in bloom most of the year.

The Caragozians didn't go hungry because, at the new ranch, they had a garden, fruit trees, chickens, a milk cow, bee hives and, sometimes, wild game. In the late summer they sometimes even had fresh trout, which was gathered by hand from the drying irrigation ditches, where the trout had washed down from the Sierra Nevada. (Nowadays the irrigation water from Pine Flat Dam is screened before being released into the irrigation system.)

Maxen spent much of her time cooking and baking on a wood stove and helping Armen in the fields. She cooked satisfying meals out of whatever was on hand. While there was an abundance of fruits, vegetables, chicken and dairy products, there were times when only Armen was served meat, since he needed strength for his heavy labor. There was no money for any extravagance, but the family did buy the ingredients for Maxen's special meals served when they had friends over for dinner.

The family celebrated holidays and special occasions with the gathering of good friends. Nothing special was planned. The Caragozians and their friends gathered around the big round table enjoying traditional Armenian food, talking and enjoying the moment, just as it had been in Maxen's childhood years.

A collection of stories that described Armenians' exuberance despite the poverty of the Great Depression won William Saroyan (celebrated writer, playwright and Pulitzer Prize winner who lived in nearby Fresno), nationwide fame in 1934. Indeed, it was the era of hard times and plenty of socializing for the young Armenian families.

No wine or beer was served but sometimes the men drank a potent liquor called *raki* in tiny shot glasses. It was made from raisins and flavored with anise. Armen made *raki* so he could offer it to his men friends. The ladies didn't drink alcohol and neither did he, except for New Year's Eve.

Each New Year's Eve, Armen poured one-fourth can of beer into a small glass and drank it all down as if it were medicine. While the family watched, he went outside and shot his double barrel twelve gauge shotgun up into the air. That done, he put the gun away and went to bed satisfied that the Caragozian family was going to have a good New Year.

Just as hospitality was the core of the Caragozian;s and their friends, so was sharing with one another. Extra fruits or vegetables from the orchard and garden were put in wooden boxes, ready to be given away to friends and neighbors. Along with the vegetables from her prolific garden, Maxen, more often than not, took yogurt or cheese to her friends. Others were given a handful of flowers from her yard and some of whatever Maxen might have baked the day before.

Armen prided himself in growing one vine of each variety of grapes that grew in California. He also had a great assortment of fruit trees. Near the kitchen window was an oversized lemon tree that was loaded with bright yellow fruit the size of large naval oranges that hung on the thick branches like ornaments on a Christmas tree. Maxen squeezed the lemons and froze the juice in ice trays so she could make lemonade and lemon pies later on. The walnut tree grew tall and provided both shade and a bumper crop of nuts each year. Growing nearby were healthy fruit trees that produced prime cherries, nectarines, plums, pears, apricots and oranges. Behind the garage were two big almond trees and an orchard of peaches. Acres of green seedless grape vines surrounded the house.

After laboring for six days, the farm families looked forward to that seventh day of rest and leisure. Sunday found them going to church, visiting friends, relaxing—and sharing those extra fruits and vegetables. After lunch, Maxen and her family either drove over to a friend's house or stayed home to welcome whoever came to visit them. Even after the telephones came to the San Joaquin Valley, friends did not call ahead—they just showed up. Just as it had been in the Old Country, there was plenty of animated conversation and laughter as they sat together enjoying each other's company.

Daughter Helene recalls simple ways they had fun as families: "We visited often and sometimes pulled pranks on a few close friends. If they were not home, we piled chairs, boxes or anything that was nearby, in front of their door so they knew we had been there. On the very top of the stacked things we placed the fruit or flowers we had brought them. They did the same thing to us when we weren't home. We would laugh about it later. We came home one Sunday to find twelve watermelons in the garage. My dad was really happy because watermelon was his favorite fruit."

In spring and summer, the Caragozians' visiting friends could expect home made ice cream, which meant that everyone took turns on the hand-cranked ice cream freezer. The flavor of the ice cream depended on what fruit was ripe at that time. Sometimes it was strawberry, sometimes it was peach and the rest of the time it was a rich delicious vanilla. There was always a tray of oatmeal or persimmon cookies or the many layered, delicate *paklava* to enjoy with the ice cream.

Friend John Atmajian, recalls his visits with the Caragozians: "I remember the wooden-planked bridge we had to drive over to get to the driveway that went to the Caragozian house. Each time we drove over it, the loosely nailed planks would rumble like the sound of thunder. This sound meant company was coming. There was no need to call ahead in those days. Making private conversation was questionable because we had several people on the same line on those old crank-type wooden wall phones."

Around five o'clock one Saturday afternoon in May, Maxen heard the sound of many car horns that seemed to be getting louder and closer. Looking out the front door, she was surprised to see a procession of over twenty cars slowly coming down their farm road to the house. Tied to the top of the lead car was a large chair.

The date was May 22, 1941. Friends and neighbors had come over for a surprise 20th anniversary party for Maxen and Armen. They brought everything that was needed for a first-rate celebration: an abundance of Armenian food, bread, many desserts that included a cake, fruits, beverages, and the gift—a handsome chair for the living room. The women quickly covered card tables with colorful cloths, laid out the mouthwatering varieties of food and soon the families were happily eating, talking and laughing. The satisfaction of a surprise party was fine, but the exuberance came from being together with good friends—enjoying the moment.

The Caragozian family worshiped at St. Sahag Mesrob Armenian Apostolic Church in Reedley. They were charter members when the small church was built in 1924. Maxen often times made the unleavened bread for communion that was served each Sunday. The church service was the same as it had been through the last 1,630 years of worship in the Armenian Church. It was a beautiful eulogy of chanting and singing, a long ritual. Restless children who squirmed in the pews were sent outside to play in the church yard.

Poverty was tolerable for Maxen. Her treasures were family and friends. Contentment filled her heart as she watched her healthy children grow in body and mind. The education that was denied Maxen was readily available to her three offspring in this new land and they liked school and learning just as she did. She encouraged them to be independent thinkers along with becoming well educated.

Maxen's own thirst for knowledge also was ever present. After everyone was in bed at night, she studied language books and taught herself to read and write in both Armenian and English. There was no time, money or opportunity to attend language school—she learned the languages on her own.

Maxen amd Armen standing in the midst of blooming bushes and colorful, fragrant flowers next to the house. She considered flowers a necessity and had plants flourishing year-round. Date unknown.

Maxen pointing to the her six foot high stand of sweet peas, a flower with perfumed scent that she grew from seed, just as she did the rest of her flowers and also the vegetables. Date unknown

Chapter Thirty Three

Life On The Ranch

The Caragozians and their friends and neighbors shared both good times and bad times. Many of them, Armenian immigrants like Maxen, were left without family and had endured similar traumas and hardships as children. Providentially, youth and optimism were on their side and they looked to the future with the assurance that things would surely be better soon.

Friends came running to help one another whenever there was a need. Son John gave an example of this as he recalled what happened when it rained while the grapes were drying into raisins:

"In September, ranchers anxiously looked up at the skies, so afraid they would see rain clouds. They needed sunshine so the grapes could finish drying into raisins. If it rained, the drying raisins would rot—a whole year's work for nothing. The process for making raisins began with the seedless grapes being picked in late August, when the grapes were sweet and ripe. Four and a half pounds of grapes dried into one pound of raisins. Grapes were picked off the vines and arranged on large wooden trays that were lined up between the rows of grapevines. It took nearly a month for the grapes to dry into raisins. Rain on these trays of grapes/raisins (unless followed by immediate prolonged sunshine) resulted in their rotting—a disaster and ruin for the farmer.

Groups of rancher friends and their families rushed to whichever farm was getting rain on the trays of drying grapes. They ran down the rows at breakneck speed, stacking and stacking and stacking the wooden trays.

The top tray acted as a roof and kept the trays with raisins below from getting wet. The people followed the rain, sometimes for miles, sprinting from farm to farm. They stacked trays until night fell."

John described the work as the fastest, roughest work he had ever done. There wasn't a choice—this was the only way to save the crops. Sometimes the crops were saved and sometimes came the calamity of drenched half-dried grapes when the rain was pouring down everywhere at the same time. (Nowadays, grape growers use paper trays, which cannot be stacked, and they buy crop insurance to protect them from rain-related losses.)

The Caragozian ranch also had an orchard of peaches that ripened in July when the thermometer reached 100 degrees. The pickers had little shade as they climbed and balanced themselves and their pails on the tall ladders, reaching out to the peaches hanging on the high limbs. Harvesting this fruit was difficult for many reasons besides the heat. Because the fruit bruised easily, the workers had to carefully place them in the pail, then climb down to the ground to put them gently into a wooden box. It took about four pails of peaches to fill one packing box. Worse than climbing up and down the ladders all day in the heat of the summer, son John recalled, was the peach fuzz that got into one's pores and produced painful rashes.

What's more, all of this work was done under tremendous pressure of time—the farmers had to get the peaches to market before they bruised or became over-ripe. After the peaches were picked, the women and girls packed them into wooden boxes. The boxes were stacked and tied onto the waiting trucks. The loading had to be done by early afternoon because it would take the truck driver twelve to fourteen hours to reach the Los Angeles produce market.

The two-hundred mile drive was very slow because of the steep, slow climbs up the hairpin curves of the road (nicknamed "The Grapevine") leading up to Tejon Pass where the ninety-horse power trucks could only manage three or four miles per hour. Son John recalled the truckers telling him that the truck cabs got so hot on the steep grades that the truckers stood on the running boards or even walked alongside the trucks, set the hand throttle, and steered the truck through the windows. This same trip now takes around four hours—new road, powerful trucks.

As was typical of small farmers in the San Joaquin Valley in the 1920s and 1930s, the Caragozians had no tractor. Instead, all of the work on the farm was done by animal or human power. With the exception of harvesting the fruit, Maxen, Armen and John did most of the work, as there was no extra money for hired help at that time.

Even when the Caragozians did hire help, they oftentimes had to re-do the work. Daughter Helene recalls Maxen going through the vineyard rows, rearranging the grapes on the raisin drying trays. The workers had not spread them out uniformly which meant uneven drying of the grapes. Many bunches of grapes were left on the vines which she picked and placed on trays. Helene also recalls Armen getting his shotgun to chase away some workers who had stolen a chicken or two from the Caragozians' hen house.

Young John began doing heavy work at age nine, such as driving the mules for plowing up the ground. The farm children helped with whatever needed doing. John earned ten cents per day repairing the wooden trays and wooden boxes. Doing a man's work as a youngster made John vow not be a farmer when he grew up. And he didn't. John graduated from Oregon State College (Now Oregon State University) with a degree in Forestry.

Their nearest neighbors were John and Mira Zaninovich, who were immigrants from Yugoslavia, spoke their language at home just as the Armen and Maxen spoke Armenian in theirs. Leaning on their shovels in the vineyards, the two farmers talked daily in broken English. There was respect and close friendship between the two families all through the years.

Armen and John Zaninovich, neighbor and good friend, pausing for a visit in the peach orchard. Date 1952.

Chapter Thirty Four

On The Move

A typical day for Maxen on the ranch in the 1930s was cooking the day's meals in the cool of the early morning, watering her flowers and garden, cleaning house, washing clothes and then moving on to a multitude of other tasks. She helped Armen in the winter at pruning time in the vineyards and during the fall harvest. Maxen placed her baby daughter (Mary, then Helene) in a big padded willow basket and off she went to the fields or orchard. In the spring and summer she worked while the baby slept under the canopy of the grape vines or in the shade of the peach trees.

Maxen always wore an apron on top of her house dress. Choosing sturdy, colorful fabrics, she sat at her treadle Singer sewing machine and made sizeable aprons with two deep pockets. That it was worn to keep her dress clean was only one of the many purposes the apron served. In the kitchen she could use it as a potholder or to wipe her hands or the sweat off her brow. Outside she sometimes stopped at the chicken coop, emerging with eggs in her apron pockets. If she went to the garden, her apron would serve as a carrier for vegetables she would need for the next meal. If she walked near the fruit trees, the apron carried a variety of ready-to-eat nectarines, apricots, plums or peaches to the kitchen. The first thing she did each morning was to put on a clean apron when she dressed.

Maxen somehow found time to sew, knit, crochet, and made exquisite needlework pieces during the day or evening. Never idle, if she sat down, there was sure to be a work piece in her hands. She made cheese, butter; and yogurt. Each year she canned hundreds of jars of peaches, plums, apricots, pears and cherries; she cured olives; she made jams from strawberries, peaches, and apricots; she dried herbs for later use.

She made *turshi* (pickles) from the vegetables in her garden. In a one or two quart jar she would stuff celery sticks, whole banana peppers, carrot sticks, whole string beans, Jerusalem artichoke pieces, garlic cloves and dill, then cover them with vinegar and hot salt water brine before putting on the lid. During the meager years, the *turshi* was made in a big ceramic crock. These pickles were usually a side dish at dinner. If, after eating dinner, you had the nerve to say *"gushdem"* (which is Armenian for "I'm full"), Maxen would suggest that you eat some *turshi* to stimulate your appetite so you could eat more.

One day a week Maxen rose before dawn to bake *lavash* or Armenian cracker bread. She had made and kneaded the dough the night before so it would be ready to roll out and bake the next morning. First she divided the dough into the shape and size of baseballs and then rolled it out with a long wooden dowel to a symmetrical large-pizza-size round which she carefully placed in a very hot oven. Since the bread browned quickly, Armen helped by taking the bread out of the oven while Maxen readied another thin round for baking. They were finished by time the children were awake.

On bread-making day, the children woke up to an ample breakfast of fresh bread with clotted cream and honey or jam, along with eggs or cheese, fruit and milk, which was the norm for other days also. Whether it was oatmeal, cream of wheat, corn flakes or eggs, there was always some kind of bread on the table. Just as it was in Maxen's growing up years, no meal was complete without bread.

Everyday dessert for the family was simple—fresh fruit or stewed fruit and pudding at times. The family snacked on natural foods such as dried fruit, almonds, walnuts, sunflower seeds and pumpkin seeds. One favorite Maxen fixed for the children was a ground up mixture of dried apricots, dates, raisins and walnuts, bound together with melted marshmallows, shaped into long rolls, then sliced; another was peanut butter and honey mixed together and used as a spread on graham crackers or cracker bread.

Yogurt, called by its Armenian name *madzoon*, was always in the refrigerator and eaten at least once a day. *Madzoon* was also mixed with molasses or it was diluted with cold water as a beverage or it was used as a topping for other food. *Mazoon* was an important ingredient in making other side dishes, hot and cold. Son John recalled that Maxen's *tahn* (made from thinned *madzoon* and flavored with minced cucumber and garlic) was a most thirst-quenching drink on summer days.

Through the 1920s and early 1930s, Maxen used a wood stove for her cooking and baking, both winter and summer. Later, a shiny white gas stove with a large oven was in place within her kitchen and her baked foods took an upward spiral quality and taste.

Chapter Thirty Five

Rememberances

*M*axen handled most any situation with nimble resourcefulness. Daughter Mary recalls:

"It was a warm Sunday afternoon in June on the ranch—a day for rest and for socializing with other families. Coming down our long dirt driveway in a cloud of dust was a brown Model A Ford with our good friends from Dinuba. After a warm welcome, my mother brought out a pitcher of iced lemonade with a heaping plateful of cookies along with an assortment of fresh fruit.

A short time later an old black coupe came slowly toward our house—this time it was the elderly priest from our Armenian Church and his wife. They liked visiting us—their faces and bodies relaxed as they settled into two lawn chairs on our shady front lawn.

It was becoming late in the afternoon, when my father said, "We want you all to stay and have dinner with us." That sounded good to everyone. My mother had a startled look on her face but she smiled and excused herself. I saw her headed to the chicken house and I heard the chickens squawk. She asked me to bring her some ripe peaches from the orchard and some corn, tomatoes, cucumbers and eggplant from the garden. I could already smell the chicken cooking when I brought in the produce. After shucking the corn and setting the table, I went outside to play.

In what seemed like a short time, my mother called us all in to eat. We sat down to a delicious dinner of chicken a la Maxen, rice pilaf, fried eggplant, corn on the cob, sliced tomatoes, cucumbers spears, homemade olives, pickles, and cheese together with Armenian bread and for dessert: hot peach cobbler."

"Maxen had a habit of humming or singing softly as she went about her work, inside or outdoors," recalls daughter Helene. "The songs were those she remembered her mother singing when she was a child. Whenever my parents wanted to have a private talk, they spoke in Turkish so we children could not understand what they were saying. I marveled that they could switch from Armenian to Turkish to English at different times. Maxen seldom had the chance to use the French language but she remembered much of it and used it during a visit to France at a later time."

Because Maxen truly enjoyed being outdoors, she didn't mind helping out with the farm work. Among other things, she was skilled in growing and propagating plants. She loved and cared for the farm animals, even the two turkeys who gobbled fiercely whenever a car came into the driveway. Despite the summer heat, Maxen wore a long sleeved shirt on top of her cotton house dress, a straw hat on her head and gloves on her hands. She was determined not to let the harsh sunlight burn her fair skin.

Their closest neighbor, when seeing her toil in the vineyards, told another neighbor several times, "That pretty Mrs. Caragozian, she should not be working in the fields." Although Maxen used no creams, lotions or make up, she remained a lovely woman, even in her seventies. She carried her five foot frame straight, her hair was pulled back in a no-nonsense bun when she was young. In her later life, she allowed herself the luxury of going to "beauty shops" for permanents and hair cuts. Always, there was an air of dignity about her, whether she was in the fields or dressed for a social affair.

Next-door neighbor Nada Stuckey recalls: "I remember most of all how pretty she was. She looked so out of place on a farm with chickens and cows and dirt. I always visualized her being a displaced queen or heiress and wished so much that she could be somewhere other than on the farm. I also remember that though she was a tiny woman, she was incredibly strong. She would hoist up the heavy cellar door like it was air."

Nada's brother, John Zaninovich remembers: "Maxen was a very beautiful person. She always treated everyone with respect, love and kindness. She set the standard for us when we were children in that she treated everyone the way she would want to be treated. I live by that rule to this day and it is our motto here at work. One day I asked her why she had a blue tattoo on the back of her hand. She said it was done by the Turks to identify her as their slave. She had tears in her eyes when she said this."

Maxen took things in stride, and didn't become disturbed easily. One thing that did bother her was Johnson grass, a tall weed that popped up everywhere, especially in the vineyards. It grew a foot or two taller than the grapevines unless it was uprooted. When Maxen saw these grasses on the ranch, she would grab a shovel, dig down to their roots, pull them up and then breathe a satisfied "Hah!" Whatever the type or size, if they were weeds, they had to be eliminated at once.

Daughter Mary recalls the day she and her parents were motoring down a country road when her father slammed on the brakes so hard that she fell off the back seat:

"When he had pulled off to the side of the road, I saw that they were both staring at a vineyard that had a great deal of Johnson grass growing around and through the grapevines. With disgust in her voice, my mother shook her head and said, *Chent mart.* (A crazy man) Doesn't he know the Johnson grass is killing his vines?

In their minds there weren't many things worse than letting one's farm get into this appalling state. If you had land, you took care of it; weeds were surely a symbol of neglect and laziness. There were no weeds showing anywhere at our place, be it vineyard, orchard or gardens."

Maxen giving calf a bucket of milk with dog Laddie at her side. Date-1950

Maxen feeding pet turkeys. Date-1950

Chapter Thirty Six

No Frills

*M*uch of what we take for granted today was unavailable to the Caragozians during the 1920s and 1930s. What little money there was went for necessities. There were no regular medical or dental check ups. Son John recalled being in pain for days because a tooth had a cavity, but no money existed for dental care. There was no air conditioning or central heat, no refrigeration except for ice boxes, no clothes dryer, no television, no supermarkets or fast food places, no credit cards. There were no disposables of any kind and plastics were unknown. Gas was eleven cents a gallon and a nice new car could be bought for $500.00, if you could afford one. There were 5 and 10 cent stores where you bought things for 5 or 10 cents or even a penny. For a nickel you could mail a letter and two postcards.

There was one thing that every home had: a radio. Radio had come into being in the U.S. just after World War I. For the following thirty years, radio broadcasts had the monopoly of the airwaves.

Family entertainment came from the few stations that were available in the area. Son John was glued to the radio when the Lone Ranger episode was on or a mystery program called The Inner Sanctum. The radio was their connection to the nation and the world. They heard in 1927 that Lindbergh had made the first solo transatlantic flight—from New York to Paris in 33 hours and 30 minutes. They were amazed to learn in 1933 of an airliner, cruising at an astounding 189 mph, had entered regular air service. They heard in 1937 that the magnificent, nearly two mile long Golden Gate

Bridge was completed and President Roosevelt had come to push the button that opened it to traffic. They were informed in 1939 that the World War II had started in Europe. On December 7, 1941 they were horrified to learn that Japanese bombers surprised the world by sinking eight U.S. battleships at Pearl Harbor, Hawaii, crippling American power in the Pacific. It was the start of a war for the United States that lasted 1,364 days.

When they were not helping on the farm or going to school, Maxen's children entertained themselves in inventive and creative ways. There weren't many "bought toys" around, and it was before the days of television or electronic games. Daughter Mary played house under the canopy of grapevines; she did pretend-cooking, making lots of mud pies and cakes. Son John and his friends played cops and robbers, shot BB guns at a target, played marbles, played baseball or went swimming in the irrigation canal. The children and their friends had fun playing hide and seek, jumping rope, climbing trees, throwing a ball over the house, chasing butterflies and dragonflies, catching tadpoles, playing pick-up-sticks, hopscotch, tag, checkers, dominoes, cards and there was the public library. Daughter Mary would check out as many books as were allowed, reading them sitting on a low limb of a fruit tree. Boredom was not a known word.

Later, as the Caragozian children and their friends became teenagers, they even water-skied on the irrigation canals. The skier would get into the canal, strap on the skis, and hold onto a rope, the other end of which was tied to the rear bumper of a car or truck idling on the canal's access road. With a jack rabbit start, the driver would speed down the road. The break-neck rides were short, though, as the skier had to let go of the rope before being towed into a bridge or a spillway.

Chapter Thirty Seven

The Made-By-John Truck

$\mathcal{T}$he family's first car was a Model T Ford. It was not an easy car to start (it had to be hand cranked) or drive, but it was the only vehicle available and affordable at that time. Replacing the Model T was a green 1929 Model A Ford Sedan that had an electric foot starter and was easier to handle. Cars at that time had no power steering, no heater or air conditioner, no seat belts and no turn signals. The family car provided needed transportation, but what the Caragozian farm badly needed was a truck.

Son John took it upon himself to take care of that need right after the family bought a new Chevrolet car. He was around sixteen years old at the time and was determined to transform the Model A sedan into a truck. He figured out just how to do it. John found a place where the back half of the Model A could be sawed off all the way down to the axle. He enclosed the passenger compartment then fashioned a flatbed in the rear. It took ingenuity, labor, patience and quite a bit of time before he finally finished his big project. John successfully launched a very unusual truck that had a hopped up engine but no doors. Before its debut John had painted in yellow letters J.C. Co. No. 5 on the both sides of the hood. Friends and neighbors applauded his creation—nobody could mistake whose vehicle it was coming down the road. .

John's truck was not only unusual, but it was indestructible. Daughter Mary recalls what happened one early summer evening when she and a girl friend were out for a drive in the truck:

"Some boys from school in a shiny, new blue car decided they were going to have some fun by scaring us. On the two lane country road, they passed us then cut back sharply in front of the truck, expecting me to brake to a stop. I didn't brake. The end result was a streak of blue paint on the front fender of the Model A and a crumpled back fender on the new blue car. The Model A didn't even have a dent—it was built to last.

The truck was used by the family for years and years. John drove it until he went to college, then sister Mary used it until she went to college. Sister Helene, though, refused to even get in it. Armen never bought another truck. He used the one-of-a-kind-Model A Ford pickup truck until he died. Son John then used it as a second car until 1959.

Much to Maxen's regret, Armen refused to let her drive a car again after her wrist was broken while she was cranking the Model T. She was involved and was badly injured in car wrecks three times while riding with friends. Those were the days before seatbelts, power steering and traffic lights—the only traffic signs were occasional stop signs. These wrecks caused serious injuries, especially to her hip. After the second injury, she lived in pain as arthritis set in and walked with a limp for the rest of her life.

Armen driving the Made-by-John Model A truck. Date-1948

Chapter Thirty Eight

The Better Years

$\mathcal{F}$ranklin Delano Roosevelt was the savior for the farmers and certainly for Maxen and Armen. He called his plans for the country The New Deal. When he came into office in 1933, his first legislative proposals were for agriculture and they were promptly passed by Congress. The Agricultural Adjustment Administration (AAA) helped desperate farmers get low-interest loans, paid for crop reduction and saw to market quotas.

On June 23, 1936, Armen borrowed $1500 from the AAA-affiliated Federal Land Bank of Berkeley; the repayment schedule was only $37.50 every six months. This loan saved the Caragozian farm. There was hope again, not only for them, but for the farmers throughout the nation.

Maxen and Armen sat close to the radio and listened intently when President Roosevelt gave his numerous Fireside Chats. Roosevelt opened his broadcast with, "My friends" then sought to reassure them. He expressed concern for them and made everyone feel as if things were going to be all right with the nation and the economy. He had the confidence of the people. He was the only United States president who won four terms in office. Roosevelt's New Deal did improve matters but did not heal the nation's problems. It did cure feelings of pessimism—people, especially the farmers, were now more optimistic about their future.

The Caragozian ranch finally became profitable in the late thirties. Farming was no longer a back breaking struggle and the family was able to put more money in the bank. Finally, Maxen and Armen allowed themselves leisure time for a few enjoyable outings.

The whole family looked forward to their yearly frolic to the Fresno County Fair. Maxen's interest was the area where there was row upon row of quart jars that contained different fruits preserved in a heavy sugar syrup. Next to them were numerous entries of colorful jams and jellies. She hurried past the pickle section to the place where she would linger—the displays of hundreds of beautiful flowers and plants. Throughout the different areas she had scrutinized the blue ribbons entries, wishing she could have entered some of her preserved fruit, jams and/or flowers.

In the meantime, Armen was in another section of the Fair admiring the handsome farm animals and the newest farm equipment. From there he would gravitate to the food stands and treat himself and his family to shish kebab-in-pita bread. Daughter Helene would be eager to move on to their last stop—the amusement park. She had impatiently waited to start her kind of fun—the Ferris wheel, fast rides and the cotton candy. Reluctant to leave, they returned home at dusk in high spirits from their great outing.

Maxen, Armen and the children also enjoyed the church picnics that were held twice a year in recreational areas or parks. Often times it would be an area along the Kings River where it was cooler and more scenic. There would be musicians playing lively Armenian music and there was a little dancing, just as it had been in the Old Country. (Armenian dancing is much like the Greek dancing—the dancers linking arms to form an open circle, moving together to the music) The mouthwatering smell of shish kebob being barbecued on long metal skewers filled the air. There was always plenty of Armenian food brought by the families to share with their friends. It was a time for togetherness; a time to forget cares and heartaches; a time for gaiety.

In 1942, Maxen and Armen decided to expand their farmhouse. They planned to add another bedroom and a bathroom plus a large room to the back of the house. The big room they called a porch, would have windows all the way around it. While the ranch's prospects improved, the Caragozians were hardly flush. On March 23, 1942, Armen and Maxen borrowed $727 from the Production Credit Association. (A lender chartered under federal law to assist farmers.) This loan was secured by the twenty acre farm and by the ranch's equipment and animals, which included:

1-Bay horse mule, 18 years
1-Black horse mule, 12 years
1-2 Horse disc
1-2 Horse plow
1-Vineyard truck
1-Single plow
1-3/8 Gang plow
1-2 Horse cultivator
1-Circle harrow
7500 wood trays
250 Sweat boxes
1-Jersey milk cow, 6 years
(Note that, as of 1942, the Caragozian's had no tractor. All the plowing, cultivating, and tilling of the soil was still done with mule power.)

Before the construction began, a basement was to be dug so Maxen would have a cool place to store the many jars of fruit she canned, along with the jams, dried fruit, honey, and assorted other things. It would be used much like the storage room her family had when she was a child.

With shovels in hand, three friends arrived one morning, ready to help Armen dig the basement. They shoveled dirt until noon, at which time Maxen invited them inside for a hearty meal. After lunch, they sat at a card table under the shade of the walnut tree and played a few hands of pinochle. They went back to digging, and Maxen came out carrying a pitcher of iced lemonade and a heaping plate of cookies. Back to the shade they went, to enjoy their afternoon snack and to play a few more hands of pinochle. It took the four men two days to dig a fourteen by fourteen foot cellar.

Armen and John, with some help, built the rest of the addition, including the big bathroom, making the outhouse obsolete.

Finally, in 1943, the Caragozians "cleared" the farm, meaning that they paid off the entire mortgage and paid nothing more. At one point, Maxen thought it wise to sell the ranch and buy another that was on the market with over twice the acreage. It would have been a very profitable undertaking but no amount of coaxing would convince Armen to go ahead with it. He remembered well the loss of the grocery store and the first ranch. Armen was afraid to take another risk and wanted everything to stay the way it was. There was no further talk about the move.

Maxen and Armen were blessed with good neighbors whose farms were within a mile's radius of the Caragozian ranch. They shared the water from the irrigation canals; they shared the workers during harvest time; they shared good news and bad. Most of them stayed on their ranches until they died or became too old and feeble to do the farm work.

Maxen and Armen. Date—1940's

Chapter Thirty Nine

Armen

*A*rmen was well liked and had many staunch friends.

He was known for his generosity, gentleness and hospitality as well his steadfast political beliefs. He was a proud member of the Armenian political party known as the Dashnaktsutyun or Dasnak. His usual day was working from dawn to dusk, stopping only for a hearty lunch Maxen had ready for him. In the heat of the summer he dipped his handkerchief in water and placed it on his head then put the hat back on. He wore his work hat year round and put on his nice gray felt hat when he went to church or to Fresno.

Two of life's greatest pleasures for Armen were farming and playing pinochle. Neighboring farmers came to the Caragozian ranch some afternoons when the heat was too intense to work in the fields. They propped their shovels against a tree and sat down in the shade to play a few hands of pinochle. The men played with gusto, whacking their cards down on the table with some choice words. They took pleasure in the rest and the fun of indulging in their favorite card game. The old card table and four well used chairs were left outside under the walnut tree all summer.

In early winter Armen's main task was pruning all the fruit trees and grapevines. Whenever he found an abandoned bird nest in the vines he brought it to daughter Helene. She delighted in getting the nests and had a sizeable assortment lined up around her room. One early morning Helene was awakened by the chirps of a baby chick. Armen had put the chick in one of the nests and placed it on her pillow.

Armen rides his Ford tractor in the vineyards.
Date- 1951

Armen stands proudly with Maxen and his children in front of the ranch house.
Date-1950

Chapter Forty

Memories Of Camping

In August, little work needed to be done on the ranch. The peaches had been picked and the grapes were ripening. Little water was left in the reservoirs, so no irrigation occurred. Even the Johnson grass refused to grow because it was so hot and dry. In August, then, many Armenian farm families, including the Caragozians took a break from the San Joaquin Valley heat by camping for most of the month in the Kings Canyon National Park, the home of the Giant Sequoias. It was one of the National Parks that came into being from part of the one hundred fifty million acres set aside as national forest lands during the administration of Teddy Roosevelt. (From 1901-1909)

In the early days, the difficult ride up to the six-thousand-foot elevation park was on a very curvy, narrow road full of horseshoe bends. One needed a strong constitution to travel to the Park.

Around 1940, the Civilian Conservation Corps (or CCC "boys") built a beautiful wide road to Kings Canyon and Sequoia National Parks, much to the delight of the folks who lived in the San Joaquin Valley. It made the parks much more accessible. The Civilian Conservation Corps had been formed by President Roosevelt as a means of stimulating the economy. It provided employment for young men who, under army supervision, built roads through the mountains and did other environmental projects.

Maxen, even more than her children, looked forward to camping in the mountains. In the early days she hired a driver with a truck to take her big tent, bedding, utensils, clothing and food to a campground near Grant Grove at Kings Canyon National Park. Although there were several campgrounds in the area, Maxen chose one of the two that was nearest to Grant Grove Village.

The Village was made up of several rustic log buildings: one housed a post office, one a small gift shop and restaurant and the third was headquarters for the National Park Service. All the campgrounds had trails leading to Grant Grove, with its ancient, towering Giant Sequoias.

The time and date of the camping trip had been prearranged among Caragozians' friends. They all looked forward to escaping the sizzling valley heat and enjoying the nearby mountains, where it was a good thirty degrees cooler. They slept in large canvas tents and did the cooking over stone fire pits that were provided at each campsite.

No flimsy cot for Maxen—she always brought her box springs and mattress from home. When the truck was to be loaded, she made sure that these two items were first to go on. She took white sheets, a bedspread, plump feather pillows, and a large rug to grace the inside of her tent.

After the better road to Kings Canyon National Park was built, Armen took all the camping supplies up the 6500 foot elevation in the Model A "truck". He loaded the bed springs and mattress first, putting them against the cab, totally obstructing his rear view. He and Maxen squeezed the tent, boxes of dishes, pots and pans, staples, food, bedding and clothes on the remaining small space. After tying everything down securely, Armen faced the challenge of taking this heavy cargo to a campground that was at a 6500 foot elevation.

Armen and the Model A moved right along with the enormous load until they approached the steep grades. Just before the steepest grade Armen revved up the engine, pressed the gas pedal all the way down and roared up the hill. The old car slowed as it climbed and conked out right before reaching the summit, rolling back down the hill faster and faster. The simple engine had over-heated during these attempts. Armen put more water in the radiator and waited on the side of the road until the engine cooled down. Once again he would rev up the engine and head up the hill, making it to the top of the steep grade on the second or third try.

People marveled at Armen's skill in being able to hold the vehicle on the mountain road as it plummeted backward down the hill. He navigated without the benefit of a rear view mirror to see the curvy road behind him.

A time or two the Model A did not make it up the grade no matter how many times Armen tried. Kind folks in cars following him would offer to take some of his load which made it possible the Model A to climb the rest of the way to the campground.

Armen remained at home, checking on the grapes' ripeness and doing the necessary farm work during the week. On weekends he came roaring up the mountain passes in the Made-by-John pickup truck, loaded down with fresh fruit, meat, eggs and milk. From the campground, his family could hear the old car when it was a mile or two away, the engine groaning loudly as it climbed the steep road. He and other farmer friends took pleasure in sitting around a card table, enjoying heated games of pinochle in the crisp, cool air of the Sierras.

Daughter Helene remembered these camping trips as the highlight of the year. The children played, roamed the trails and generally ran around unsupervised. Mothers did not worry about them. The tantalizing smell of food cooking on the fire lured the hungry kids back to the campsite. The only downside for the children was that walk to Wilsonia, a little village that was a mile from the campground, to take a shower every so often.

These were the times that Maxen could leave her work load and relax. She took other trips but here she had the pleasure of being with many of her good friends. She was in good health, her children were playing nearby— and she was in the grandeur of the Sierra Nevada mountains.

Even in the mountains Maxen wore an apron over her dress while she cooked over the campfire. (Women did not wear slacks in those days) She was teased about keeping every thing so neat and clean around the campsite and sweeping the inside of her tent twice a day.

The men arrived from the Valley by Friday afternoon so it was an early supper that evening and the next. After the meal men, women and children congregated around someone's campfire. They sat on folding chairs, sometimes listening to those who played music on traditional Armenian instruments such as the *oud,* similar to a lute or guitar, and the *duduk*, a clarinet. Most famous for his expert *duduk* playing was Hovagim Hagopian, who played with gusto and was in great demand at weddings and other celebrations.

Other times, the campers told family stories, Old Country tales, and laughed at new jokes. During the day they took short walks along the trails or played pinochle or just sat and read at the campsites. This brief respite in a beautiful setting and away from farm work brought great pleasure.

Once a week the National Park rangers gave a campfire program at the amphitheater that was within walking distance of the campgrounds. The older people took homemade wooden canes to walk the trail and the youngsters ran ahead excitedly so they could be there first. They were armed with flashlights and warm jackets to wear when the evening became dark and cold. Greeting them at the amphitheater was a very large bonfire in a stone pit next to the small wooden stage. Strains of western music filled the air. They sat on long smooth logs imbedded in the dirt, happily waiting for the evening's entertainment. At last the Park Ranger, neatly dressed in his uniform and matching hat, walked onto the small stage to present the program. The campers were seldom disappointed. First, it was a sing-along, with the words of familiar songs shown on the big screen, followed by a brief talk about Kings Canyon National Park and perhaps a short movie.

An hour later they were all walking back on the dark trails illuminated only by their flashlights, shivering in the cold night air. Program night was the only time adults and children stayed up late. The rest of the week everybody went to bed shortly after dark and rose with the woodpecker at the break of day.

The crisp, sweet mountain air brought Maxen special joy. It brought back memories of her idyllic childhood years in mountainous terrain of her village. She drank the cold clear water from the campsite faucets remembering the cold streams of melted snow of her earlier days. These camping trips were the happiest times in Maxen's adult life.

Chapter Forty One

Fall And Winter

$\mathcal{J}$t was still hot but tolerable when the Caragozians returned from their mountain vacation. In a week or two the grapes would be ripe enough to be picked for drying into raisins. Armen used a special piece of equipment on the tractor to smooth and flatten the soil between the rows of grapevines where the trays of grapes would be placed to dry in the sun. The workers arrived in due time and the harvest began. The peaches had already been harvested in July. Weeks later the raisins were sold and the late fall and winter work began. Armen repaired the ranch equipment, sharpened all his pruning shears and replaced or straightened any wobbly wooden posts to which the vines were attached.

Maxen canned the last of the fruit and vegetables and stored them away. She also dried her herbs to use during the winter. Some of the mature herbs, vegetables, and flowers were set aside until their seeds were collected. Maxen dried the seeds before placing them in labeled envelopes and put them all into a sturdy cardboard box, ready for her spring gardens. Maxen and Armen made *basturma,* a beef filet which was coated and cured with spices and salt and air dried. At special times later on it was sliced very thinly and served as a pungent appetizer.

During the colder November and December, Armen pruned the fruit trees and then the grape vines, leaving the strong shoots for the following year's growth. Maxen followed him in the vineyard with a ball of twine and a sharp knife to cut the twine. She twisted and quickly tied the remaining shoots onto the thick wires that were strung from post to post to the end of each row of grapevines. It was tedious work to prune and securely tie the vines to the wire but totally necessary. It would guide and ensure the vines new spring growth so that the grapes would have plenty of needed sun and remain well above the ground.

It took weeks to finish and when they did, Armen and Maxen picked up all the pruned branches of the trees and the spindly vines trimmings off the ground. They piled and burned the smaller pieces but saved the longer and bigger pieces to fuel their woodstove and the *ojak*. (The Armenian word for brick barbecue) Nothing was wasted.

Chapter Forty Two

The World War II Years

*I*ronically, the outbreak of World War II on September 1, 1939, which brought misery and death to millions of people in Europe and Asia, was a boon to the American farmers. Prices rose dramatically for such crops as raisins and peaches, both of which were growing on the Caragozian ranch. Raisins and especially peaches could be dried or canned so they were in high demand for military rations as well as civilian use. Also, the war had destroyed much of European agriculture so the American farmers had little competition.

Armen was glad that his son John had talked him into putting in a peach orchard instead of the grapevines he had planned for that space. The demand for peaches was so great that, one year, the buyer supplied his own pickers—Armen sold the peach crop on the trees, making a very handsome profit.

High prices for the crops helped many San Joaquin Valley people. In 1943, for example, son John and his close friend, Johnny Chakerian, earned $1000 by going to various ranches where they picked grapes and sold the "second crop." (That is, fruit remaining on the vines after the main harvest) John used part of his earnings to buy Maxen a beautiful gold watch. It was the first watch she had ever worn and she cherished it the rest of her life, mainly because her son had given it to her.

The boon was not only for the farmers—problems with economy and unemployment were reduced. At the beginning of the war seven million

Americans were still out of work. Not only did they gain employment but eight million more people went to work, some for the first time. Armen, along with the other farmers who were struggling in the 1920s and hard hit by the Depression, was seeing his earnings triple.

Immediately after Pearl Harbor, the draft of men between eighteen and thirty six years of age began, putting sixteen million young men into uniform. Maxen was relieved that her son was only fifteen but saw her friends' sons going to war.

A flag with a blue star hung in the front window of each home that had a soldier fighting in the war. The Gold star meant that your son or husband had died in the war. Good friends, the Torosians, had all three sons in battle overseas—they had two blue starred flags and one flag with a gold star.

Patriotic Americans bought forty nine billion dollars in war bonds. Even children saved their pennies to buy twenty-five-dollar war bonds. Son John put aside his nickels and dimes, accumulating enough money to buy several of them.

The United States had changed. It was the age of new developments and advances in science and medicine. Plastics developed as did synthetic rubber and industrial capacity rose as more factories were built. California was no longer known only for farm products—industry had arrived. Farm laborers left the rural areas and headed to the cities to look for an easier life.

There was also a change in Maxen's life. In 1944, at the age of thirty nine, she became an American citizen. Her husband, Armen, had become a citizen nine years earlier. She never missed a voting day and kept up with the political happenings in California and the nation.

One of the Caragozian's neighbors, the Okinos, were involved in another drama after war was declared against Japan. Daughter Mary's classmate, Sharyn Okino recalls: "What a rude awakening upon arriving at school Monday morning to be called Japs and seeing the other Asians (Chinese and Korean) wearing signs stating, `I am an American`. Up to that time I certainly considered myself as American as anyone else. Suddenly we had a curfew of 8 pm. Two of my brothers could not attend their own graduation from grammar school and high school."

Writing in the Fresno Bee newspaper, California native David Masumoto said, "In August of 1942, all Japanese-Americans living in the Western

United States were exiled to relocation camps. During internment, they were shamed: losing property, belongings and respect. Some Armenians in our Valley saw a connection between our internment and their own family histories of the Genocide. They insisted that their families take care of the Japanese-American farms: they knew what it was like to lose everything."

Chapter Forty Three

Transitions

*J*oyful celebrations were held all over the United States when the war ended. Actually, War II had two endings. Victory in Europe, called VE Day, was May 8, 1945. Victory over Japan, called VJ Day, was August 15, 1945. Americans celebrated twice as their soldiers came back home.

Migrant Mexican workers came to the Caragozian ranch to harvest the crops in the 1940s and thereafter. Farming was quite profitable by then. Their ranch was producing heavy crops and receiving good prices for them. There was an assortment of good farm machinery in the big gray barn and the Chevrolet car was in a new garage.

Maxen was concerned for her son, John, who joined the United States Army before the war ended in 1945. He was sent to Ft. Benning in Georgia for basic training. John was to be part of the invasion of Japan. There was no invasion because after the atomic bomb was dropped on Hiroshima and Nagasaki, Japan surrendered. John still shipped out to the Pacific and saw occupation duty in Japan and in Korea.

Maxen was terribly worried about her beloved son being overseas. Her thoughts and prayers were about him day and night. Daughter Helene remembers her mother's tears dropping on the bread dough she was kneading while her lips moved in prayer. Her apprehension eased only when her John was honorably discharged and came back to the United States in 1947.

Maxen corresponded with both her Uncles Kegham and Melik through the years. There was a steady exchange of family pictures in the letters. Every year she put together a large assortment of the choicest dried fruit and nuts and delicacies. They were destined to be sent to her uncles. She carefully packed all of it in big wooden boxes, without a fraction of an inch to spare. After daughter Mary or Helene printed the addresses on top of the boxes, Armen made a special trip to the Reedley post office to put them in the mail that very day.

Uncle Kegham's daughter Diane remembers their "goodie box" always arriving just in time for Thanksgiving—crammed full of nuts, dried apricots, raisins, home baked Armenian goodies, which were eagerly devoured by the family. Kegham's son Edward recalls, "When this special box arrived it was never opened that day—it was saved until the entire Aghjayan family gathered together. We ceremoniously opened the box and everyone would enjoy Maxen's treats."

Maxen's last trip to Boston was in 1948 when she had a joyous reunion with Uncle Kegham and Uncle Melik and their families. Two years later, she agonized over her beloved Uncle Kegham's untimely death. He died in March of 1950 when he was fifty three, leaving three young children without a father.

The only survivor of Maxen's mother's family was an uncle who had migrated to Florida before the Armenian Genocide in 1915. He had changed his last name from Arslanian to Arslan. They saw each other only twice—once when he came to California to visit her and once when she traveled southeast to see him in Orlando. He was a balding blonde haired man with the same vivid blue eyes as Maxen's. A dignified looking, slight of build man—the family resemblance was there. She lost him a year after Uncle Kegham died.

Maxen had not been able to choose her partner nor time of marriage; she also had no control over its end. Widowed at age fifty-one, Maxen met this challenge like she had all others in her life. With the help of her son John she carried on the farming. Even though he lived some distance away from the ranch, her son John came almost every weekend to do the heavy work.

She decided to lease the land for the following years but kept an eye on everything that was going on. Maxen was heard telling the renter, "You see those are weeds under the vines? Plow again!" While known as gracious lady with a quick sense of humor, she was a demanding taskmaster when it came to the upkeep of the ranch.

In 1960, she thought it best to sell the ranch and move three miles to the town of Reedley. Maxen had lived and worked on a ranch for thirty nine years; now was the time for a change. Many of her good friends had already made the transition from farm life to living in Reedley so she would not be lonely. Through the years she had been shopping, banking and attending church in Reedley while living on the ranch.

With her daughter Helene she made the move, leaving behind over a hundred blue canning quart jars in the basement and all farm equipment in the barn. Anything and everything that had to do with farming stayed right there. All her gardening tools, seeds, seedlings, cuttings and the large assortment of flower pots went with her to the town.

Maxen standing proudly beside son John and daughters Mary and Helene. Date-1946

Maxen visiting with her uncles Kegham and Melikof.
Roslindale, Massachusetts, 1948.

Maxen in Roslindale with her beloved Uncle Kegham in 1948, her last visit with him before his sudden death at age fifty three. He single-handedly saved her life and, against great odds, succeeded in bringing her to the United States.

Chapter Forty Four

Town Living

$\mathcal{M}$axen's new residence was a white frame house on Linden Avenue in Reedley. The quiet street was lined on both sides with large shade trees. A spacious lawn graced both the front and back of her house.

The backyard grass decreased and gradually disappeared, as Maxen increased the size of her vegetable and flower gardens. Within a short time the lawn was all but gone. She reasoned that instead of the "worthless" back lawn, she would put the space to good use by planting vegetables and fruits. She grew tomatoes, zucchini squash, green beans, carrots, lettuce, Jerusalem artichokes, Swiss chard, eggplant, carrots, green and banana peppers, corn, cucumbers, black berries, strawberries, parsley, and all the herbs she needed for her cooking. The yard's perimeter had grapevines and loquat, orange, lemon, nectarine, apricot and peach trees.

Maxen's green thumb was legendary. In her back yard flower garden were brilliant masses of saucer-size dahlias; sweet peas that grew six feet tall, staked and leaning against the side of the garage; rows of zinnias and carnations in vivid reds, oranges, pinks and yellows. A variety of fragrant roses were planted under the bedroom windows on the unseen side of the house. A lone bird of paradise plant she placed in the ground as a sprig grew to five feet in diameter and four feet high.

Her neighbors laughingly said that Maxen could put an old bare stick in the ground and it would have blooms the following spring. They knew their friend Maxen could not exist without flowers and her vegetable garden.

Eventually the original back lawn had shrunk to a three-foot-wide strip, which, as her grandsons recalled, could be mowed with exactly three passes with Maxen's old push-type lawn mower. That tiny strip was left there mainly to separate the flower garden from the vegetable garden. It also served as a pathway through the back yard to the clothes line and the back alley. A few of her neighbors liked to come through the back gate, so they could enjoy the beauty and fragrance of the flowers. They walked the narrow strip of grass to her patio where they happily visited as they sipped coffee and enjoyed some of Maxen's pastries. Maxen would not let them leave without a bag of fresh vegetables and a bouquet of just-picked flowers.

Another reason Maxen's place was different and unique was the very tall Redwood tree growing in her back yard. The first year she was in Reedley, she had stuck the three inch seedling in the ground and although Redwoods are generally slow in growth, this one shot up remarkably in a year's time. It continued growing lofty and green, becoming a landmark with its top standing high and proud above any other tree in her neighborhood. She loved that tree because it reminded her of Kings Canyon National Park but grumbled because it shaded some of her garden area. Her grandchildren had fun picking up the small, hard cones that fell off the Redwood tree.

Every Memorial Day, Maxen took buckets of her best flowers to the cemetery. Her first stop was always her daughter Mary's grave where she wept as she lovingly placed the most beautiful of the flowers beside the tombstone. The rest of the flowers were divided amongst the grave sites of her husband and her friends. Doing this took nearly the entire day because she paused at each grave, sadly reminiscing before moving on to the next one.

Maxen's back patio was a jungle of vigorous potted plants she had to cut down to size every few weeks. She propagated African violets by sticking one leaf in soil. She had dozens of violet pots in an array of colors basking in just the right exposure to the sun on her dining room table. They were moved only when she was expecting guests for dinner.

It seemed that Maxen had managed to condense her twenty acre ranch into one city lot. She rose at dawn, just as she had on the ranch, to weed and water the gardens, enjoying the quiet coolness of the morning. She allowed no weeds in her flower beds and vegetable gardens, and, thank goodness, no Johnson grass was to be seen anywhere around.

During the rest of the day she was busy baking, cooking, canning , cleaning, sewing on her foot-treadle Singer sewing machine, knitting, crocheting and doing her exquisite needle work. She knit numerous afghans, crocheted countless colorful potholders and made dozens of intricate lace doilies. She made aprons, table cloths, place mats: she knit scarves and socks. She gave them all away.

Grandson John recalled Maxen at night sitting under a lamp, in the dim yellow light of a 60 watt bulb, doing needle work so fine that he could not see the thread. She wore no glasses until her mid sixties when she begrudgingly bought a pair that had a slight magnification.

In the evening, Maxen also kept up with the news and politics by reading the Armenian newspaper and listening to evening newscasts on television. She was dismayed with the political scene. She emphatically said many times, "Before, we had dedicated statesmen in our national government who had vision for our nation and had the honesty to work for its well being. We now have name calling, bickering politicians whose chief interest is being reelected." She was also disturbed at the decline in moral standards as evidenced by vulgar talk and women wearing skimpy clothing on television.

Most important, before going to bed each night, Maxen sat at the well lit kitchen table and read her well worn Armenian Bible. She knelt down beside her bed, head bowed above her clasped hands in meditation and prayer before going to sleep.

Maxen was content with her life in town. She didn't drive, but friends stopped by to take her to do her errands and to shop. Her phone rang often and she welcomed the many visitors who came by to visit. Sarah Bergthold, who lived in the house across the back alley-way from Maxen, walked over for a short visit nearly every day. The two women sat either on the patio or at the kitchen table where they talked about the local or national news, their families, and their aches and pains. Then they switched to fun topics, ending their visit with laughter.

Because her younger daughter Helene lived in the next town of Dinuba, Maxen was able to be with three of her eight grandchildren. She disciplined them just as she would her own children, and they didn't seem to mind at all. They were happy to be there because there was always a variety of delicious food to eat and they didn't run out of things to do at "Nana's" house.

One day Maxen was hanging out clothes on the line when a parakeet landed on her shoulder and refused to fly off. The grandchildren were delighted with the colorful bird as it sang songs and repeated many words. The bird stayed happily in its cage near the kitchen for many years and was a source of enjoyment for Maxen. The grandchildren gave her a little white gosling the Easter after the parakeet died. By the end of the summer she had a very large goose who wanted to come in the house each time she opened the back door.

Grand daughter Krista said: "Not a week goes by that I don't think about Nana's influence on my life and my choices. In one memory I'm standing beside Nana as a little girl as she waters her lawn. I listen to her hum a gentle and familiar Armenian song. I can still see her walking up her driveway toward the backyard, her weighted gait (pain in her arthritic hip made her limp) not slowing her speed or determination. As I watch, I see another set of legs and feet following suit. What a sight—Nana and Herbie, the goose were quite a team. I don't remember ever seeing such a spoiled pet in my life."

Chapter Forty Five

Going Abroad

$\mathcal{F}$orty-eight years after leaving France for her journey to America, Maxen went back to Europe. She was sixty-two when she decided that if she was going at all, this was the time to do it regardless of her many health problems. When her son John offered to accompany her, the plans were quickly made, and off they went.

They visited Athens, Greece then Istanbul and Ankara in Turkey. There was no point in visiting her village. After militia and mercenaries had killed all the Armenians in the village, the Turks and Kurds had moved into the vacant houses. Only the forlorn stone shell of the Armenian Church was left as a reminder of whose territory it had been for hundreds of years.

They traveled to Beirut, Lebanon to visit Armen's youngest sister, who was born after he had left for America and his sister had corresponded through the years but he had never seen her. By happy chance, Maxen and son John arrived there when Armen's niece was getting married. They had the opportunity to meet all the family at the wedding.

After a brief visit to Israel they flew to Marseille, France for a poignant visit with her old friend. Maxen had corresponded with her French friend since she came to America and knew the address by heart. They cried and embraced when they saw each other again—forty eight years before they had both been fifteen years old. Her friend took a ring off her finger and put it on Maxen's: a gift of love. They held hands as they happily reminisced their good times together long ago, laughing as if they were teenagers once again.

Chapter Forty Six

Atlanta Garden

$\mathcal{M}$axen tackled most any task with a combination of remarkable physical strength and determination. On her first visit to her daughter Mary's home in Georgia, she brought an assortment of seeds from her own garden. She had decided to plant a vegetable garden for her daughter and family.

The day after Maxen arrived she walked out to the back yard and eyed all the tall pine trees that shaded the area. She threw up her hands and said, "How can you have a garden with all these trees—you need sunlight!" Maxen hurried to the tool shed and located a hand saw, an ax and pruning shears. With no hesitation, this petite little woman felled six good sized pine trees.

During the course of the day she also cleared the under growth that would be the garden area. That very afternoon, her son-in-law dutifully hauled off all the debris when he came home from work.

The next day she attempted to till the ground but the hard, red Georgia clay would not budge under her shovel. Determined to plant that garden, she invited the next door neighbor over with his tiller. (She rewarded him later with a good dinner.)

After getting the ground just right with top soil, peat moss and fertilizer, she planted her seeds, watered them and was content in that her daughter would soon have fresh vegetables. She was nearly sixty years old at the time.

Chapter Forty Seven

Unique Cuisine

$\mathcal{M}$axen was a gourmet cook and served organic food a half century before "gourmet" or "organic food" was in anyone's vocabulary. She would have no part of "bought" baked goods. Whether it was a wonderful dessert, appetizer or a main dish—Maxen produced it seemingly with no effort and often times at the spur of the moment.

When her children had friends over, their wish for snacks was quickly granted. If they craved potato chips she quickly peeled a couple of potatoes, sliced them thinly, crisped them in hot oil, salted them and a bowl of delicious chips emerged. If they wanted sweets, there was plenty of fruit candy or thin sheets of fruit *bastech*. (Today's commercial fruit rollups) The most popular snack was one or two of the rich variety of fresh fruit.

Most everything Maxen used in her cooking was home grown and natural. She baked and cooked with whole wheat flour, whole grains, yogurt, assorted vegetables and fruits. There was a minimum amount of refined food on her table. She used whole wheat flour combined with some unbleached white flour for her bread making. Maxen cooked hearty, delicious stews using mostly chunks of lamb and sometimes beef with the different vegetables. Thick lentil soup, chicken soup, and meatball soup (*kufteh*) was standard for winter lunches. Her homegrown herbs, onions and garlic were a must for seasoning her main dishes. Maxen used very little fat in her cooking and when she did, it was olive oil or butter. She disdained margarine of any kind.

Maxen was delighted when her children and grand children brought friends to visit and to dine. Those who picked at their food were quickly forgotten, but those who ate heartily were fondly remembered. Before they left Maxen's house, children, grand children and friends were given various things to take home, be it baked goods, leftovers from dinner or fresh fruit. As they took their leave, Maxen stood at the doorway, smiling and waving goodbye—still wearing her apron.

"Precious thoughts of Maxen always had to do with her ever present smile and her actions showing one thing: love," tells family friend, Armen Kandarian. "She and my mother, both quiet spoken ladies, would spend a pleasant afternoon talking about children and church activities while I indulged myself in the delicacies on the table. As we said our goodbyes, Maxen busily loaded us down with some of everything she baked, cooked or preserved. Generosity was her middle name."

Neighbor Johnny Zaninovich tells of eating a lot of meals at Maxen's kitchen table. "I ate *shish kabab,* chicken, *pilaf, lavash,* sweet breads, pastries and many more delicious things. I loved the *rogeg (*walnut and grape juice roll). I loved everything she made but I couldn't get used to the *madzoon. (*Yogurt) When I was in the Army she sent me packages of goodies she had made," he said.

Neighbor Nada Stucky fondly recalls how she and Helene could smell the wonderful aroma of good things cooking in Maxen's kitchen the minute they stepped off the school bus. "We would hurry in and sample whatever it was she was making. My greatest joy was getting a big piece of Armenian cracker bread, smearing it with mayonnaise and putting sliced fresh tomatoes on top then eating it with gusto. She always had the biggest and healthiest garden—she grew everything." Nada said.

Grandson John recalled that Maxen's breakfasts were a special challenge. "They included fried eggs. If you asked for one egg you got two. In addition there was bacon, homemade cheese, fruit, two or three different kinds of homemade jams and—not least—three or four kinds of homemade sweet breads. If you somehow managed to eat some of everything, except you neglected one of the breads, Grandma noticed. She kept track like an accountant and asked why you did not eat that particular bread. If you managed to survive breakfast and had just pushed yourself away from the table, you then heard her rattling around the pots and pans, getting ready for lunch," he said.

Dispensing loving hospitality was inborn in Maxen and it was her belief that warm hospitality and sharing food at her table went hand in hand. Since Maxen's expertise in the kitchen was known far and wide, her friends knew they were in for a wonderful treat when they came for lunch or dinner. And they knew that they better come hungry because she did not believe in skimpy meals. The table would be laden with an abundance and variety of beautifully prepared Armenian food.

Maxen always noticed when someone was not eating. She passed the food around to them again and invited them to help themselves but she ate sparingly.

A high point of Maxen's hospitality was a special company dinner. The menu was diverse and everything was made from scratch. Doing this took enormous time and effort in the way of shopping, cooking, baking and cleaning up but family and guests repaid this effort by eating heartily.

The main appetizers (the Armenian word for appetizer is *messe)* were *yalanchi,, basturma,* cracker bread, string cheese, olives and pickles that were made from assorted vegetables. *Yalanchi* is a moist and delicious appetizer made from her canned grape leaves. The leaves were wrapped around a seasoned mixture of onions and rice sautéed in olive oil, cooked and drizzled with lemon juice when cool.

A special dinner took two days to prepare. The menu would include many of the following Armenian dishes:

Lamjoon—(similar to pizza), a thin pancake size round of yeast dough that was topped with seasoned ground lamb, tomatoes and chopped parsley and baked in hot oven.

Boerags—baked *phyllo* triangles filled with cheese and parsley and sometimes seasoned meat.

Sarma—home canned grape leaves wrapped around a mixture of lean ground lamb or beef, rice, herbs and spices, simmered to perfection.

Dolma—banana peppers, tomatoes, slender eggplant or small potatoes filled with the same mixture as *sarma,* covered and simmered together.

Pilaf—a rice dish always served with a meat made by browning very thin noodles (vermicelli) in butter, adding rice or cracked wheat *(bulgour)* and chicken broth, simmering until done.

Souboreg—somewhat akin to cheese lasagna with Maxen's pasta rolled out thinly and individually dipped in boiling water. It was layered with cheese and parsley and baked.

Green beans, okra or eggplant—lightly seasoned with herbs and cooked in various ways.

Cucumber, sweet onion and tomato salad—laced with olive oil and a mild vinegar.

Cut up fruits—whatever was in season.

Lastly, always on the menu and most important—*Shish kebab* that was marinated overnight, skewered and cooked outside in a traditional Armenian brick barbecue pit, *ojhak,* using grape stumps or wood for fuel. Two kinds of bread rounded out the feast.

Chapter Forty Eight

Tempting Desserts

*N*o company dinner was complete without dessert (*anoushaghon*) and coffee. There would be a choice of at least two or three desserts. If they were not all eaten, the desserts would be packed up and sent home with the guests.

Most of Maxen's desserts and pastries were delicious concoctions of fruits and nuts but she was well known for her standard desserts: lemon meringue pie, cream puffs, persimmon cookies, *khorabia (*Armenian cookie) and the delicate desserts that were made using *phyllo* dough.

Two desserts*, paklava* and *burma,* were made from Maxen's phyllo dough. After making the dough to just the right texture, she divided it into dozens of golf-ball sized rounds. Using a yard-long wooden dowel, she rolled out sheet after sheet of phyllo dough, dusting each with cornstarch to keep them from sticking to the table and to each other. Actually, she rolled out five at a time. First the ball shaped dough was quickly rolled out to pancake size disks, then were stacked five high with cornstarch between them to keep them from sticking. She rolled them out tissue-paper thin to perfect circles about sixteen or more inches in diameter.

Grandson Ted recalled Maxen rolling out the phyllo so thin he could read a newspaper through them. The desserts she made from these sheets were delicate morsels of perfection. She made and mailed the sheets of phyllo to her daughter who lived in Atlanta. She wouldn't hear of a daughter of hers baking desserts and *boerags* with "tough store-bought" phyllo.

Golden delicate *Paklava* was and is made by fitting forty sheets of phyllo sheets into a baking pan, layering them with chopped walnuts or pistachios and melted, clarified butter, then cutting it into triangles before baking. *Burma* was and is made by rolling up the phyllo like a cigar with nuts inside and melted butter on top. After baking and while still hot, a thin syrup of sugar, water and lemon juice was poured over them. Both the *paklava* and *burma* remained delicious for weeks.

Maxen's dessert expertise also included *roegig*, made with thickened grape juice and whole walnuts; *bastegh*, thin, dried sheets of thickened grape juice or pureed apricots; *khorabia*, a delicate shortbread Armenian cookie; candied figs and candied apricots. She made up many unique recipes for candies, cookies, pies, cobblers, and cakes using fresh or dried fruit, walnuts and almonds. Maxen made these and scores of other delicacies but she seldom ate them.

Grandson John describes how Maxen made *roijig:*

Several dozen fresh, big walnut halves were strung together with a needle and heavy thread, and several such strings were dipped in boiled, thickened grape juice and hung vertically from a rack to dry. Over several days, the dipping and hanging process was repeated and repeated until the walnuts were coated with about a half an inch of dried grape juice. The strings resembled long, lumpy, beige candles. The middle threads were pulled out and the long *roejigs* were dusted with powdered sugar or cornstarch and wrapped up tightly for storage. When serving, the *roejigs* were cut crosswise into half-inch thick slices.

Dessert was accompanied by regular coffee or a strong coffee, often termed Armenian coffee or Turkish coffee. Finely ground coffee beans and sugar for Armenian coffee were boiled with water in an hourglass shaped brass pot called a *jazveh.* After sipping the hot coffee down to the fine grounds in the demitasse cup, the cup was turned upside down in the saucer and turned three full times clockwise so the grounds could trickle down inside the cup. Then Maxen would "read your fortune" by looking at the grounds inside the cup. This bit of entertainment concluded a two-or-more-hour feast.

Chapter Forty Nine

Confident Ways

After moving to town, Maxen continued her mid-summer, one day trips with friends or family to Grant Grove in Kings Canyon National Park. Her children and grandchildren will never forget those happy times.

Her Grandson John remembers well:

"The trips involved loading the car the night before with utensils, firewood, food and the like, then starting for Grant Grove at dawn the next morning. Upon arriving, Maxen put her apron on and started a fire in one of the stone and cast iron fireplaces while we unloaded the car. First things first: the coffee pot was put on, then the *katah*, sweet breakfast bread, was warmed up and peaches or nectarines were sliced. Finally bacon and eggs were fried in a large black iron skillet.

After breakfast was finished, Maxen put a large metal pan on the fire to heat dishwater. She did not believe in flimsy paper plates—we ate on the china plates she brought along and the picnic table was covered with a print tablecloth."

"In the middle of the day everyone relaxed. The children and grandchildren might hike to the Big Trees (where the Giant Sequoias grow) or down to the Village. By early afternoon, Maxen re-started the fire. She adeptly prepared and served a mouth-watering shish kebab dinner which included rice pilaf, *sarma*, green salad, *lavash, boureg,* fruit and a couple of her desserts."

"Once again, she packed up everything and down the mountain we came just as it was getting dark. It was the ending of a memorable day for the whole family. These big breakfasts and lunches, eaten outside in the crisp mountain air with the scent of the pines and the gurgle of the nearby creek, were incomparable."

The only recipes Maxen used were for dessert and breads which she might have found in the newspaper or a magazine. Her practiced eye knew which recipe would be worth trying. She put these clipped recipes in a shoebox and seldom used them again. Although she did not care for sweets, she enjoyed making them to give away and to serve to friends who dropped in.

Maxen's electric mixer was rarely used—she made everything by hand, using an egg beater, whisk or wooden spoon to mix the ingredients. She used a long wooden dowel the diameter of a broom handle, rather than the typical rolling pin, to roll out thin sheets of *phyllo* dough and the dough for *lavash,* Armenian cracker bread.

She didn't believe in using a dishwasher, either. "I can do it better and quicker in the sink," Maxen said. She used the dishwasher as storage cabinet for plastic containers and a few staples. Once, by accident grandson Ted switched on the dishwasher, soaking everything stored inside.

At the meat market Maxen avoided the already-ground beef or lamb. Instead, she selected a lean beef steak or roast and maybe a leg of lamb. Once home, she removed all the fat and gristle then cut the meat into whichever size pieces she needed. With her well used metal hand grinder, she ground up some of the lean pieces to her liking and cubed the rest for her stews or kebabs.

Maxen's children never saw pork on their table. There were two reasons for this. One—she had not eaten pork as a child and was not going to eat it now. Second, and more important, she had read that many pigs were infested with a worm that caused something called trichinosis in humans. There was one exception of her ban on pork and that was bacon—it was a must for company breakfasts. She reasoned that bacon was perfectly safe since no worm could possibly survive in meat that had been cured and then fried crisp. Her taboo of pork remained through the years.

Those who knew Maxen were in awe of her talent and her ability of creating beautiful, tasty food, whether it was breakfast, lunch or dinner or merely dessert with coffee. Where did she learn to do this? She was orphaned when she was ten and had not watched her mother or grandmother cook. She once said that she had learned the basics of cooking while helping the Turkish woman during the years she was their slave.

After she married, she became an expert cook and baker by adapting her own tastes and variations to the traditional dishes. She grew a great variety of herbs in her garden and used them skillfully. She did not compromise on the ingredients or the time that went into her cooking and baking.

Many of the customs of Maxen's homeland were left behind and mostly forgotten but there was one important one that was carried over. Cooking and baking Armenian food connected her to family traditions.

Just as her mother and grandmother had done when she was a child, she put a silver dime in the *katah*, sweet bread, on special occasions such as Easter and Christmas. As before, whoever had the dime in their piece of bread was happy and excited because it meant good luck all year long. Her daughters watched their mother make *katah* and have continued this tradition and the preparation of many of her Armenian dishes.

Her grandchildren and great grandchildren have continued the custom of the egg cracking contest at Easter.

Times and places changed but the continuity of customs such as these and the genial hospitality passed down through the generations remain as a solid link to Maxen and the family ancestry.

Maxen bestowed love upon family and friends with her kind generosity and gracious hospitality, with delicious meals that required hours to prepare and by giving away the products of her exceptional talents—the delicacies created in her kitchen, the exquisite needlework and handwork of her own design and bright flowers and fresh vegetables from her garden.

Chapter Fifty

Maxen's Children

Maxen was a gentle protector and the mentor of her children. She was careful not to belittle them but on the other hand, she very seldom praised them and never bragged about them. She did not tolerate laziness. Without question, Maxen expected her children to work, to realize their capabilities and give their best to whatever they were doing.

Maxen didn't need to tell her children to be polite; to be kind and hospitable; to be humble; to be strong in the face of hardships and disappointments; to turn to God for strength and guidance; to be compassionate to those in need; to know the worth of good friends; By being a living example of these and other beliefs and behaviors, Maxen had set the standard from the very beginning for both her children and those who knew her.

Her three children were aware of the incredible sacrifices she had made for their well being. In addition to being a devoted mother, they felt that she was their greatest friend and loved her deeply. The years of adversity had taken their toll on her body, but her mind was vibrant and keen until the very end.

Son John was an "A" student all through elementary and high school. He graduated as valedictorian from Parlier High School and was awarded a football scholarship to Saint Mary's University in California. He attended only one semester before enlisting in the Army. After his discharge he attended Reedley College for one year and went to Oregon State College (now Oregon State University) on the G.I. Bill. He graduated with honors in 1951 with a bachelor's degree in Forestry. He married and had two sons: John and Ted.

Daughter Mary also graduated from Parlier High School with high scholastic honors, held offices and was the school's representative to Girls' State. Mary received her associate arts degree from Reedley College and a bachelor's degree in Home Economics from the University of California at Davis. (Father Armen saw no value in girls going to college and did not support Mary at all.) Maxen, on the other hand, believed that her daughters must have at the very least a college education. Maxen send her money on the sly. Mary worked her way through college and was also helped by a scholarship. Mary became a high school teacher, married and had three children: Alan, Dana and Judy.

Daughter Helene also graduated from Parlier High School in high standing and held various offices. She graduated from Fresno State University with a bachelor's degree in nursing. Helene earned a Master's degree from the University of California at Davis and received an additional degree to become a nurse practitioner. She married and had three children: Steven, Krista and Michelle.

Maxen lived to see her oldest grandchild, John Caragozian, graduate Cum Laude from Harvard Law School. Her other seven grand children went on to careers in law, medicine, advertising, accounting and financial management, teaching, banking, and environmental affairs.

Maxen lived her later years in much pain but still tended her prolific gardens and did her beautiful handwork. She was content knowing that her children loved one another and were blessed with families and good friends of their own, that they lived in a free country, had good educations and did not have to suffer the adversities of her generation.

Her aspirations for her children had been fulfilled.

Chapter Fifty One

Maxen's Legacy

$\mathcal{M}$axen died on March 6, 1984, on her first-born daughter Mary's birthday.

Maxen's life's journey had been one of faith, courage, strength, and devotion to her family and friends. She did not allow bitterness to warp her mind despite the fact she had experienced the death of her entire family as a child along with the trauma of being an orphan and a slave; despite the fact she lost her beloved first born, endured years of poverty and later, poor health.

Maxen walked her life's journey in quiet dignity and courage; she chose the path of deep faith and optimism regardless of the harsh circumstances of her life. The essence of Maxen's individuality—love, patience, kindness, generosity, integrity, extraordinary talents, sharp intellect, and quick wit— made her both a role model and an inspiration to those who knew her. She was dearly loved by all.

Maxen leaves behind the rich heritage of the ancient Armenians and the priceless legacy of faith and love.

To honor their mother/grandmother and her lifetime desire for education and her quest of excellence, Maxen's family established a perpetual scholarship in her name. The first Maxen Aghjayan Caragozian scholarship was awarded in 1985.

I sought the Lord and he answered me, and delivered me from all my fears.
Psalms 34:4

Maxen Aghjayan Caragozian

Maxen with Mary, John and Helene in the late 1970's

Chapter Fifty Two

The Armenians

𝒯o better understand the meaning of Maxen's story, one must have some knowledge of the Armenian people. The following is a very brief summary of this ancient race that dates back nearly three thousand years.

Armenia is one of the oldest civilizations known to us. Through most of the more than three thousand years of its existence, its people have spoken one language and for the last seventeen centuries have worshipped the same god in the same way in its national church. The Armenian people have always clung to their culture, traditions, language and religion.

The country itself has been known by many names: by the Armenians themselves, Hayastan; by the Persians and Russian, Armeniya; by the Romans, Arminia; by the Turks, Ermenistan; in the Bible, Minni. Historical data of the Armenians dates back to 1250 B.C. The Armenians were carving their own niche in the history of man at the dawn of civilization. Their original homeland, called the cradle of civilization, was in the plains of Mount Ararat that extended from the Caucasian mountains in the east to the Euphrates River in the west.

At its zenith, historic Armenia stretched from the Black Sea to the Caspian Sea and from the Mediterranean to Lake Urmia which is now in Iran. During the 1022 years of self rule there was a long line of nobility of kings, queens, princes and princesses, along with great prosperity. The greatest period as an empire was in the first century before Christ (the era of Julius Caesar) under the rule of Tigranes the Great. It is said that Armenia's ideas and institutions during this period helped shape the history of man and formed the basis of western thought. Armenia was a strong, thriving nation during the first five centuries A.D.

What little the world knows of the Armenian people is more for their sufferings than for their accomplishments. Their turbulent history reflects an endless chronicle of rise and fall, triumph and tragedy.

Through the centuries, Armenia was a bridge for international commerce between Oriental countries and the West. Armenian merchants traveled to remote countries so set up trading posts and carried on international trade. They exchanged their goods using caravans on land and chartering ships to reach faraway places. In addition to great quantities of agricultural products, merchants exchanged goods of raw silk, spices, horses and mules, wine, dyes, oils, rugs, textiles and vast amounts of metals such as gold, silver, iron, copper, tin and zinc. Historian Jacques de Morgan maintains that the iron industry started in Armenia twenty centuries before Christ. Discoveries have shown that the world's first steel furnace was built in Armenia nearly 3000 years ago. Armenia was also the first to domesticate the horse. Their horses were famous and prized though out the Near East for many centuries. Their beautiful handmade rugs were sought far and near.

Armenia became the first Christian nation in the world in 301 A.D., while most of the world continued to worship pagan gods. The fifth century was known as the Golden Age of Armenian literature, the time of great literary achievements. This was about the time the Roman Empire was disintegrating and the Dark Ages were settling in Europe. In contrast, the Armenian culture was reaching its highest peak. During this period monasteries were the centers of learning, with the written word directed into countless manuscripts, epic poems, songs and books. When the Bible and the Holy Scriptures were translated into the Armenian language, a historian wrote that God became an Armenian-speaking God.

The Armenians became a creative people in the following centuries despite political upheavals and extreme hardships. They built handsome churches and cathedrals, developed beautiful native music and art, and wrote great poetry and literature.

Because Armenia, with its riches, was in a strategic position at the crossroad of much of the known world, powerful rival nations quarreled over the right to dominate her. Sadly, Armenia's vital location between the East and

West was a political misfortune for them. Ancient Armenia became a buffer state and was overrun by neighboring empires.

The Egyptians, Persians, Assyrians, Romans, Arabs, Seljuk Turks, Mongols, Russians, and Ottoman Turks—all at one time or another have sent their armies to invade the land. The ravaging and desecrating of towns and villages were recorded as far back as 714 B.C. when the King of Assyria invaded. The geographical boundaries of Armenia flowed like mercury through the Near East, usually at the will of the conquerors. As a result, five different Armenian kingdoms have existed for a thousand of the last 2,500 years.

The Armenians, being fiercely nationalistic and independent, somehow survived, regrouped and retained their identity through the hundreds of years when other nations dominated portions of their nation. Against great odds, the Armenians successfully asserted their individuality and upheld their national heritage and their religious beliefs throughout their long, tumultuous history—a three thousand year narrative of defiance and survival. Most of Armenia's ancient neighbors—the Babylonians, the Assyrians, the Medes, Parthian, and the Byzantines—have all disappeared as races.

The Sejuk Turks swept into Greater Armenia in the eleventh century, driving great numbers of the Armenian people out of their homeland. Their property and assets were confiscated as they fled to Georgia, to Iran, to Syria and to Cilicia, where Lesser Armenia arose—sometimes called Little Armenia. This kingdom and the Armenian culture flourished for three centuries (1080-1375) on the Mediterranean Sea, south of the Tauras Mountains. The area, which is now southern Turkey, was overrun by the Mameluks (Egyptians) in the late fourteenth century. Over the centuries the Ottoman Turks reached their height of power, taking control and completing their conquest of Armenia in 1395. The last Armenian king died in France in 1393.

Their beloved land, where Maxen's people lived for thousands of years, was in the hands of the Turks. They were Christians in a Moslem world and did not have the rights of citizens. They were in an Armenia that did not belong to them. The Armenians owned land and businesses but had no voice in government and could not own weapons. They were heavily taxed and treated with contempt and cruelty to which they had no recourse.

The Armenian people themselves have moved and been moved about so often that their imprint as industrious and capable traders, artisans and professionals has been left in areas throughout the world. No matter which corner of the earth they fled to, they quickly adjusted to their new circumstances, became loyal citizens, and in time, leaders in politics, industry and business.

National Geographic says: Peaceful, hard working, intelligent, religious, family oriented, Armenians have become a great, though little known, success story—but not in the land of their origin.

Wherever they went, they built their church—the same distinct architecture and the same service as they had done for centuries. Sadly, in many cities the Armenian population was gradually integrated into the existing culture or perhaps died out, leaving behind empty churches as the only evidence of their having lived there. Churches, more than 1,000 years old, are still standing today because of their distinct architectural features and construction.

Regrettably for the dwindling Armenian race, thousands upon thousands have already been assimilated into the various countries to which they fled during the various oppressions in their native land. At this time, Armenians continue to be absorbed into the different cultures where they have made their homes, thus reducing the already small numbers of Armenians left on earth.

Forced assimilation occurred through the hundreds of years of Turkish conquest of Armenia. In 1895-96 alone, 100,000 Armenians, most of them very young boys, were taken into both Turk and Kurd Moslem families and the same number of young Armenian girls was forced to become concubines or wives. Their children would be Moslems, thus strengthening their race.

There were once 100,000 square miles of land in Armenia. Today only ten percent of this ancient land is in Armenian hands—the rest of it is occupied by the Turks, the Azeri Moslems, and Iran. The only part still called Armenia was within the Soviet Union but is now an independent state. The Turks have what was Western Armenia and the Azeris control the larger parts of the Armenian provinces of Nakhicheven and Karabagh. There is no trace of Armenians around Mt. Ararat where their history began and where Armenians lived for over two thousand six hundred years.

The great wealth of history of this ancient culture remains buried in the ruins of their ancestral homeland.

The oldest Christian church on earth is still holding services in the small town of Echmiadzin which is near Yerevan, the capitol of Armenia. It was built in 303 A.D. by St. Gregory, the Illuminator, who brought Christian faith to Armenia. The ancient cathedral is within a walled enclave along with a seminary. Most Armenians scattered throughout the world look at this citadel as their spiritual center. Yerevan is a city older than Rome, founded eight hundred years before Christ.

"There was a time when courageous people of the past built a nation with an unbridled devotion to human liberty. They carved a niche in the history of the human race and in the process became one of the most dignified people of this world. These industrious people of the past sewed the fabric of a society with the highest standards of human values and for 2,600 years fought valiantly to uphold those values."

"There was a time when Armenia was a land of milk and honey, beauty and culture with laughter, songs, the smell of wheat and sun filled harvest. There was also a time when this was a land of oppression, bloodshed, and terror. Despite the paradise lost, the history of this people remains imperishable,"

From THE ARMENIANS, by John M. Douglas

Chapter Fifty Three

The Armenian Genocide

$\mathcal{T}$he true story of the long, sad struggle for survival by the Armenian people is not known to most of the world. The following is a brief writing of the barbaric, systematic extermination of the Christian Armenians by the Muslim Turks—the unacknowledged first Holocaust of the twentieth century.

In his memoirs, American Ambassador to Turkey in the early 1900's, Henry Morgenthau wrote:

> The new political party, the Young Turks, were really an irresponsible party. In 1914 Talaat, along with Enver and Djemal, were the three Turkish chieftans who dominated the Turkish Empire. "Turkey for the Turks" was now Talaat's controlling idea. Djemal was a man for whom assassination and murder were all part of the day's work. He was cunning and remorseless to an extreme degree and he despised the subject people of the Ottoman Empire. They decided to exterminate them wholesale and Turkify the empire by massacring the non-Moslem elements.

> Thus began the murder of a nation—the destruction of the Armenian race. Unspeakable atrocities and torture, the height of cruelty and injustice, were used to destroy the Armenians. The Kurds helped with the butchering, both in the villages and in the deserts.

The sadistic orgies of which these Armenian men and women were the victims can never be printed in an American publication. Whatever crimes the most perverted human mind can devise and whatever refinements of persecution and injustice the most debased imaginations can conceive became the daily misfortunes of this devoted people.

I am confident that the whole history of the human race contains no such horrible episode as this. The great massacres and persecutions of the past seem almost insignificant when compared with the sufferings of the Armenian race in 1915. The Turkish government said they were deporting the Armenians to new homes. My failure to stop the destruction of the Armenians had made for me a place of horror and I found intolerable my further daily association with men who were still reeking with the blood of over a million human beings. I returned to America.

The order from the ruling officials for systematic destruction of all the Armenian villages and   communities in the Ottoman Empire was successful. Of the two and a half million Armenians living in the Ottoman Empire before 1915, a million and a half were exterminated. The Armenian people had been thoroughly uprooted and dispersed; their wealth, homes, lands and churches plundered.

The atrocities had begun in a big scale on April 24, 1915. Armenian leaders, intellectuals, writers, lawyers, educators and members of the Turkish Parliament were taken from their homes and slaughtered. The Turks then rounded up and murdered the Armenian doctors, skilled artisans, priests, merchants and any other professionals. With the leaders gone the Turks began the massacre of more than a million and a half men, women and children. One half million Armenians fled, being subjected to the horrors of deportation. The other million and a half died in mortal agony of savage butchery and torture or they suffered the slower, more prolonged agony of starvation and thirst as they were driven into the Syrian dessert to die. Rewards were given to Turks and Kurds who killed the most Armenians during this bloodbath.

In villages and cities the process was simple—get a list of the Armenians, kill them, do a body count, find the ones that were missing and kill them, cross out their names, burn the title deeds, and take the land, businesses, homes and property.

This barbarous slaughter was given a formal name: The Armenian Genocide. It was carried out between the years of 1915 and 1918. After a year or so of calm at the end of World War I, the atrocities were renewed between 1920 and 1923 on the few Armenians remaining in Turkey.

After the genocide and the confiscation of the Armenian wealth and property, the Turks quickly demolished all traces of the Armenian culture that had flourished for thousands of years—the great churches with their unique architecture, the cemeteries, the monasteries, libraries, archives and the ancient historical sites. There is never any mention by the Turks of the Armenian race ever having lived there.

The only city in the Ottoman Empire where Armenian people and their churches survived was Constantinople (now Istanbul) because the city was very visible to the rest of the world. Even in that city, the leaders and professionals were quietly taken away and murdered at the beginning of the Genocide.

No one came to aid the Armenians because the world was focused on World War I. There was no television coverage, no news media at that time, so the Turks kept it quiet and denied that any such thing had happened. They still deny the fact that they drove two million Armenians from their homes and that a million and a half Armenians were murdered or forced to the Syrian Desert to die.

Turkey succeeded in killing and scattering to all parts of the world a small race of Christian people and no one seemed to have noticed.

The massacre and attempted obliteration of an ethnic race in Turkey was not acknowledged by the world. Even today the shame of the Genocide has never been admitted by the Turks. Instead, the Turkish government variously alleged that the survivors and witnesses exaggerated, that the Armenians merely were World War I casualties, or that the government itself did not conduct the Genocide. These allegations pale, however, against the numerous authentic writings by witnesses to the mass murders along with photographs of the sadistic atrocities. Also survivors, many of them orphans such as Maxen Aghjayan, have told of the horrific events.

The world has recognized the holocaust of the Jews in Nazi Germany and destruction of other groups on the grounds of ethnic origin in Uganda, in Bosnia, in Rwanda, in Liberia, in Sudan and in Iraq. Turkey fervently denied the Genocide so the world turned its back and forgot. Of course history is written on the side of the winners. Turkey robbed the Armenians of their homeland and their history, virtually eliminated them as a race and took no responsibility for it.

Recently, the Armenian Genocide has gained recognition in Europe but the United States continues to placate the Turks by rejecting any official commemoration of the Genocide. A resolution to make April 24th a commemoration of the Genocide of the Armenians was presented to Congress in October of 2000. Turkey threatened to cancel U.S. business dealings and to close the U.S. bases in their land if this resolution was passed. Turks living in the United States went on a rampage of phone calls and letters to the politicians to stop the resolution. Even after eighty-five years, the Turks did not want the world to know of their murder of a race of people. In the Senate forty-eight senators voted for it and fifty said no to the day of remembrance. In a press release the Speaker of the House stated, "I believe that the Armenian people suffered a historic tragedy and this resolution was a fitting condemnation to those events."

Turkey manipulates and distorts history, giving no mention of the Armenians as the long time inhabitants of the land. Turkey not only massacred the Armenians but destroyed everything associated with the Armenian culture. There is no   acknowledged trace of anything Armenian in Turkey now and there is no mention of Armenians at any time, any where. Turkish authorities have deliberately destroyed all Armenian antiquities. They have also prohibited archeological digs for study of this ancient race on land where Armenians had lived for thousands of years.

In the following words, Pulitzer Prize winning author William Saroyan conveys the sentiments of many Armenians concerning the Genocide:

"We shall never forfeit the feeling of suffering and remember our martyrs. The Turk has been named the villain. I don't believe in villains. What we hated was the government that deceived and betrayed us and behaved in an inhuman way with us. In the end there must be a diminution of hatred in favor of understanding. And so, what the Armenians ask, and rightly, is an acknowledgement by the present Turkish government of a crime against humanity and appropriate behavior to supplement that acknowledgement."

Maxen Aghjayan's sentiments were quite different.

Her family, relatives and everything dear to her were cruelly swept away by the Muslim Turks. She was forced into slavery for four years, sleeping in the cold with the dog at night. These traumas in Maxen's young life were stamped permanently in her mind and body.

The Turkish government said it never happened. Their denial of the Genocide caused her additional pain.

She could never forgive the Muslim Turks.

Epilogue

The descendents of Maxen, Yezegiel, Melik, and Kegham gathered together for the first Aghjayan Family Reunion. It was held at Plimoth Plantation, Massachusetts on August 7, 2004.

Yezegiel's son, Hachig (Hutch) Aghjayan initiated, planned and hosted the joyful Reunion. He summarized the struggle, the hope and the achievements that the family members embody:

"As witnesses of the example offered by the Pilgrims who came to this great country before us, we descendants of Avedis and Nazely Aghjayan are celebrating today almost a century of the transplantation of our family from an old country setting, which left much to be desired, to a new country, where dignity has been afforded us and a chance to prosper gifted to us by our enterprising forebears to whom we must always be grateful as those pilgrims of our family who were willing to set out to a new land without benefit of language or resources but possessing an indomitable spirit of which we have become blessed beneficiaries."

Listen to me, you who follow after righteousness, you who seek the Lord; look to the rock from which you were hewn and to the quarry from which you have been dug.
Isaiah 51.1 (New Berkeley Version)

Aghjayan Family Tree

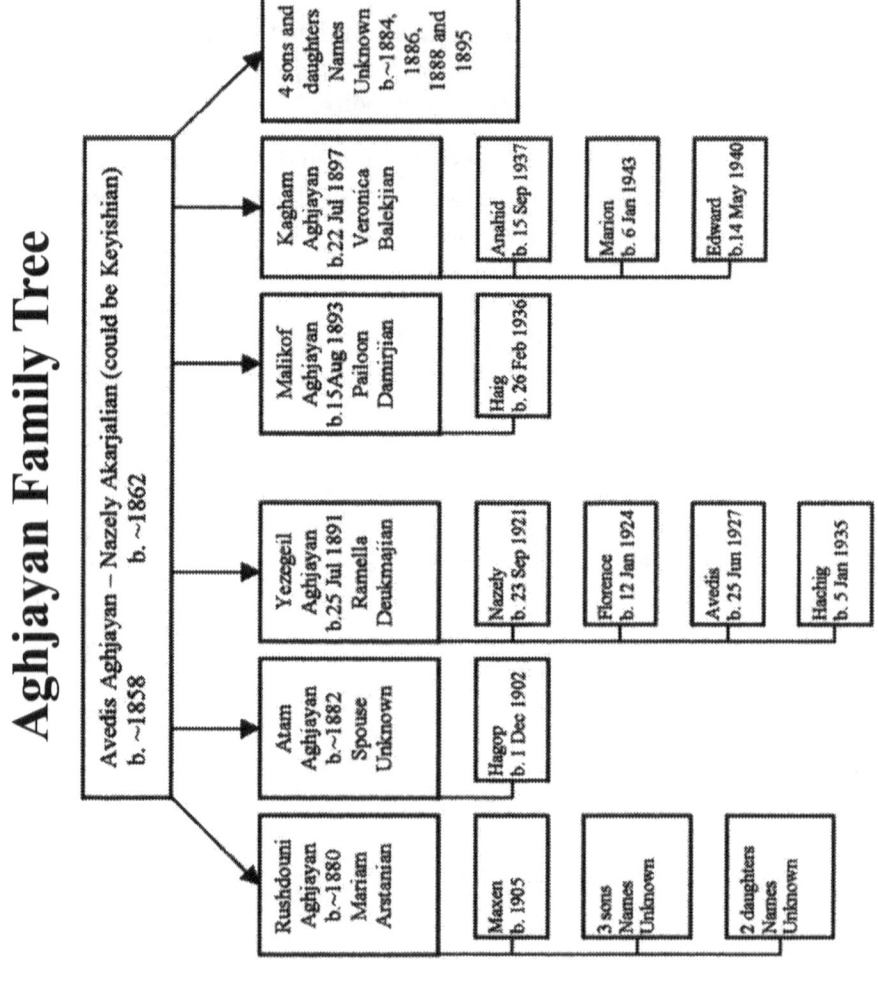

Maxen's Family

Maxen Aghjayan/ Armen Caragozian*
Married May 20, 1921

Mary (died at age 8)

John Caragozian/Tony Pletchmy
  John S.Caragozian/Janie Schulman
      Emma Caragozian
      Max Armen Caragozian
  Ted Caragozian/Cathy Magruder
      Sara Magruder
      Kellen Magruder

Mary Caragozian/Gordon Thompson
  Gordon Alan Thompson/Brenda McPherson
      Amy Thompson
      Marie Thompson
  Dana Maxine Thompson/Judson Alden
      MaryAllyn Alden
  Judy Thompson/Michael Ross
      Avery Ross

Helene Caragozian/Barrett/ Hure/ Glenn Webb
  Stephen Barrett
      Christopher Barrett
  Krista Barrett
  Michelle Hure

*Armen's parents—Kalouste and Gullie Caragozian
  (Possible spelling: Karaghuesian)
He was one of eight children.

Kegham's Family

Kegham Aghjayan/Veronica Balekjian
Married December 4, 1935

Anahid (Diane) Aghjayan/ Arthur Bassett
Franklin Kirk Bassett
Michaela Bassett
Lawrence Arthur Bassett
Glen Thomas Bassett
Stephen Richard Bassett
Vincent Kegham Bassett

Marion Aghjayan/Geloran/Killion
Richard Arthur Geloran/Elizabeth Peritzian
Stephan Richard Geloran
Vincent Kegham Geloran

Edward Aghjayan/Janet Mary Chencus
Douglas Joseph Aghjayan
Cynthia Louise Aghjayan/Mark Yusin
Thomas Yusin
Nicholas Yusin
Kenneth Edward Aghjayan

Melissa Jean Aghjayan

_____

Melikof's Family

Melikof Aghjayan/Pailoon Demirjian
Married February 18, 1934

Haig Aghjayan/Shooshie Der Manuelian
Pauline Aghjayan/ Ara Getzoyan
Dalita Getzoyan

George Aghjayan/Joyce Guimont
Christopher Haig Aghjayan
Sarah Lillian Aghjayan
Kathryn Margaret Aghjayan

Yezegiel's Family

Yezegiel Agjayan/Ramela Deukmejian
Married November 20, 1920

Nazely (Natalie) Aghjayan/Vartan Nranian
John Aghjayan/Georgia Daley
Keith Aghjayan/Debbie Williams
Andrew Jackson Aghjayan
Phillip Aghjayan/Tamela West
Jamie Aghjayan
John Aghjayan
Lauren Aghjayan
Andrea Aghjayan/Raji Taweel
Elias Taweel
Helena Aghjayan/Benitez
Brandon Benitez
Ryan Benitez
Adam Benitez

Florence Aghjayan/ Azagalian
Lynn Aghjayan/Tim O'Leary
Devon O'Leary
Conner O'Leary

Caitlin O'Leary
Logan O'Leary

Avedis Aghjayan/ Mary der Movsesian
Stephan Aghjayan
Karen Aghjayan/Vinnie Robinson
Aveda Robinson
Casey Robinson
Gregory Aghjayan

Hachig Aghjayan/Virginia McCabe
Christopher Aghjayan/Joanne Garneau
Elizabeth Aghjayan
Nicole Aghjayan
Christy Aghjayan
Jeffrey Aghjayan/Linda Marshall
Justin Aghjayan
Christohper Aghjayan
Alexander Aghjayan
Allison Aghjayan
Jill Aghjayan/David Vang
Rachel Vang
Rebecca Vang
Andrew Vang

The Armenian Alphabet

Ա ա **Ш** այբ ayp	Բ բ **Բ** բեն bpen	Գ գ **Գ** գիմ gkim	Դ դ **Դ** դա dtah	Ե ե **Ե** եչ yech
Զ զ **Զ** զա za	Է է **Է** է eh	Ը ը **Ը** ըթ uht	Թ թ **Թ** թո tto	Ժ ժ **Ժ** ժէ jeh
Ի ի **Ի** ինի eenee	Լ լ **Լ** լյուն lyoon	Խ խ **Խ** խէ kheh	Ծ ծ **Ծ** ծա dsah	Կ կ **Կ** կեն gehn
Հ հ **Հ** հո ho	Ձ ձ **Ձ** ձա tza	Ղ ղ **Ղ** ղատ ghad	Ճ ճ **Ճ** ճէ jeh	Մ մ **Մ** մեն men
Յ յ **Յ** յի he	Ն ն **Ն** նու noo	Շ շ **Շ** շա sha	Ո ո **Ո** վո vo	Չ չ **Չ** չա tcha
Պ պ **Պ** պէ beh	Ջ ջ **Ջ** ջէ cheh	Ռ ռ **Ռ** ռա rra	Ս ս **Ս** սէ seh	Վ վ **Վ** վեւ vev
Տ տ **Տ** տիւն dyoon	Ր ր **Ր** րէ reh	Ց ց **Ց** ցո tsoh	Ւ ւ **Ւ** հիւն hyoon	Փ փ **Փ** փիւր pyoor
Ք ք **Ք** քէ keh	** ԵՒ** Yev	Օ օ **Օ** օ o	Ֆ ֆ **Ֆ** ֆէ feh	

Armenian Proverbs

Eenkuzeenk seeraharoghu murtsagits choonenar
The man who falls in love with himself has no competitors

Khmitchkeen megu lava, yergooku ga pava, yereku tsav a
One drink is good, two is enough, three brings sorrow

Amen mart khent eh. Khelku an e vor eer khentutiunu gu
Everybody is crazy. The normal person is the one who covers up his insanity

Inkzinku kovoghu, geeuna zibli goghovu
Whoever praises himself falls into the trash can

Negh meedku line lezoo oonee
A narrow mind has a broad tongue

Kesh lezoon adzelien soor a—dzagadzeen tegh chuga
An evil tongue is sharper than a razor—there is no remedy for what it cuts.

Khosku ardzat-- lurootunu vosgee
Speech is silver—silence is golden

Mod turstseen heroo yeghpormen lav eh
A close neighbor is better than a distant brother

Hegheghu gerta, avazu gu muna—turamu gerta, kusgu gu manaMartu gerta, anoonu gu muna
The flood passes, the sand remains—Money goes, the purse remains. Man goes, his name remains

Hooysu aghkadeen hatsn eh
Hope is the bread of the poor

Armenian Terminology

I am Armenian—-*yes hye em*

Yes—aee-*yo* No—*voch* **Please**—*khun-trem*

Where—*oor* **Why**—*een-choo* **Who**—*ov*

Thanks—shn*or-ha-ga-loo-toun* **When**- *yerp*

How-*ench-bes*　　　**Listen**—*muh-deeg-ereh*

Brave—*Kach* **Alas**—*Vai*　**Mr.**—*Barron*

Mrs.—*Digin*　**Come in**—*hra-me-tsek ners*

Who's there—*ov-eh*　**Where is it**—*oor-eh*

You are welcome—*see-rove*

Excuse me— *ne-ro -ghoo-toohn*

How is everything—*eench-ga-chee-ga*

Let's go—*yer-tahnk*

How are you—*ench-bes-es* **Not bad**—*kesh cheh*

I am fine—*lahv em*　**How long**—*vor-kahn aden*

How far—*vor-kahn-heh-roo*

When can we go—*yerp gur-nahnk yer-tal*

That's enough—-*herika*

WORDS OF ACTION:

To run—*vah-zeh*

To work—*ahsh-kha-dee*

To walk—*kah-leh*

To swim—*lo-gha*

To play— *dh-gha*

Greetings and Salutations

Hello—*parev*

Good morning—*pah-re-loo-ees*

Good evening— *pa-ree ee-ree-goon*

Good night—*kee-sher-pah-ree*

Good bye— *mu-nahk pah-rov*

Come again—*no-rehn hrah-meh-tsek*

I'll see you again—*guh des-nuh-veenk no-rehn*

What is your name—*ah-noo-nu eench eh*

Merry Christmas—*shnor-hah-vor- dzu-noont*

Happy Easter—*shnor-ha-vor zah-de*

Happy New Year—*shnor-ha-vor-dah-ree*

Come visit us—*Hrah-meh-tsek meh*

Go in peace—*Ertauk Parov*
        (When a friend is leaving)

Books and Manuscripts

Armen, Garbis, *Historical Atlas of Armenia*
(Armenian National Education Committee 1987)

Avakian, Arra S.,*The Armenians in America*
(Lerner Publications Co. 1977)

Babessian, Havaness Krikor, *Atlas of Historical
                                    Armenia (1933)*

Elizabeth Bauer, *Armenia: Past and Present*
(Armenian Prelacy 1981)

Bryce, Vincent, *The Treatment of Armenians in the
                            Ottoman Empire 1915-1916*
(His Majesty's Stationary Office 1916)

Caragozian, John L., *My Autobiography*
(Manuscript ca. 1947)

Chahin, M, *The Kingdom of Armenia*
(Croom Helm 1987)

Chalabian, Antranig, *Armenia, After the Coming of Islam*
(Privately published 1999)

Douglas, John M., *The Armenians*
(J.J. Winthrop Corp. 1992)
Durant, Will, *The Age of Faith*
(Simon and Schuster 1950)

Ferrell, Robert H. & Richard Natkiel, *Atlas of American History*
(Fact On File 1990)

Filian, Reverend George, *Armenia and Her People*
(American Publishing Co. 1896)

Gall, Alice C., *In Peace and War, A Story of Human* Service
(Thomas Y. Crowell 1941)

_____, *Great Events of the 20th Century*
(Readers Digest 1977)

Kurkjian, Vahan M., *A History of Armenia*
(Armenian Benevolent Union 1958)

Morgenthau, Henry, *Ambassador Morgenthau's Story*
(Doubleday, Page & Co. 1919)

Nansen, Fridtjof, *Armenia and the Near East*
(Duffield & Co. 1928)

_____, Oxford Encyclopedia of World History
(Oxford University Press 1998)

Papajian, Sarkis, *A Brief History of Armenia*
(Privately published 1974)

Tashjian, Nouvart, *The Priscilla Armenian Needlepoint Book*
(Priscilla Publishing Co. ca 1928)

Tcholakian, Arthur, *Armenia—State/People/Life*
(Paradon Publishing Co. 1975)

_____, *Treasured Armenian Recipes*
(Detroit Women's Chapter, Armenian General Benevolent Union 1949)

Villa, Suzie Hoogasian, *Armenian Village Life Before 1914*
(Wayne University Press 1982)

Articles

The Armenian Library and Museum of America
Presentation: *Forgotten Heroes, The Armenian Legion and the Great War*, 2001

National Geographic, *The Proud Armenians,* June, 1978

National Geographic, *Armenia Reborn,* March, 2004

_____, The World Book Encyclopedia, *Map Reference* (Volume 1, "Armenia" (1965)

Other
Television Documentary: *The Hidden Holocaust—the Armenian Genocide*

www.ingramcontent.com/pod-product-compliance
Lightning Source LLC
Chambersburg PA
CBHW061402280526
45784CB00001B/339